The Right Opinion:
A Heretic's Voice from the
Ivory Tower

The Right Opinion:
A Heretic's Voice from the Ivory Tower

Dr. Mathew Manweller

iUniverse, Inc.
New York Lincoln Shanghai

The Right Opinion: A Heretic's Voice from the Ivory Tower

iUniverse books may be ordered through booksellers or by contacting:

iUniverse
2021 Pine Lake Road, Suite 100
Lincoln, NE 68512
www.iuniverse.com
1-800-Authors (1-800-288-4677)

Because of the dynamic nature of the Internet, any Web addresses or links contained in this book may have changed since publication and may no longer be valid.

The views expressed in this work are solely those of the author and do not necessarily reflect the views of the publisher, and the publisher hereby disclaims any responsibility for them.

ISBN: 978-0-595-46675-7 (pbk)
ISBN: 978-0-595-90970-4 (ebk)

Printed in the United States of America

Contents

Foreword

I am an academic. This is NOT an academic book. There are no footnotes, parenthetical citations, or bibliographies. If that's what you were looking for, return this book immediately to wherever you bought it and get your money back. There is, however, some humor and lots of exaggeration. Most of it is based on my recollections. Some of those recollections are clouded by age, some by beer.

I do enough academic writing. I wanted to do something different this time. I wanted to write a book that people would actually read. Maybe even enjoy reading. I can't say that about any of my other books. In part, I wanted to tell a story. A story about what it's like to be a conservative in academia. But I also wanted to write a book about ideas. Ideas matter. I think Lincoln and Reagan understood that better than any of our other presidents. I know it may sound strange, but we academics don't get to write about ideas that much. We do research. We run regressions. We report the results. But we rarely get to simply say "I have an idea." It turns out that Harvard University Press doesn't care that I have ideas. They want research.

I have not used anyone's name. I'm still pretty young. Most of my colleagues and just about all my friends are still alive. I'll have to wait until they start dying off to write the really good book. And I don't want to get sued.

So this book is part story, part ideas. It's the story of how an obscure academic, teaching at an even more obscure university, became, for a very short period of time a state, national, and international figure … and then became obscure again. It's a story about how someone with no intentions of becoming politically active did exactly that. But mostly, it's a book about ideas. My ideas. I promise that there are no graphs. No statistics. No mathematical formulas. Just ideas and opinions from an academic trapped in the ivory tower.

I should also note that although I currently teach at Central Washington University this book represents my impressions of academia based on my experiences at many universities and colleges. The danger of writing a book like this is that some people may assume all my stories, escapades, and misadventures emanate from one place. That is not true. I have been a student or an instructor at the following institutions: University of California—Irvine, University of Idaho, Whitman College, Boise State University, University of Montana, University of Oregon, and Central Washington University. The events and academic pathologies I write about come from my conglomerate experiences at all these institutions, not just my current place of employ. So, if you read something that angers you, please do not call the public relations department at CWU. It may save you some time and me some headaches.

Along those same lines, writing about where you work, or have worked in the past, is a lot like writing about family. You love these people, but the stories are still funny and worth passing on. I can say from my experiences so far, Central Washington University is an excellent place to send your children for an education. It is staffed with dedicated administrators, committed teachers, and the school provides excellent opportunities for hard working students. Regardless, there is something to be said about being the "black sheep" of the academic family. I'm about to say them.

1

My Life As A Heretic

I am a heretic. That's not too unusual. The world is full of heretics. But what makes my situation unique is that I am a heretic in a place where, by its most cherished traditions, there can be no heretics. Academia. Academia is a place that prides itself on being separated from the rest of the unrefined world. In academia everyone is welcome. There is no racism. No sexism. No homophobia. It is place where all ideas are given a reception. So, in a place where there is no dogma, there can be no heretics. But I am one none the less.

You see, tolerance is a funny thing. I thought tolerance meant that one was supposed to be patient with people who held ideas different than your own. Don't believe in the same religion as I. That's okay. I'm tolerant. Hold different views about marriage. Don't worry. I'm tolerant. But in the rarified halls of the ivory tower, tolerance has a single caveat. You can be gay. You can be an atheist. You can be a transvestite. Heck, you can be a gay transvestite that worships groundhogs. What you cannot be is a Republican. There are some things that simply go too far. Those who are open-minded can only forgive or overlook so much.

I am a Republican. I am also an academic. I am very lonely.

I learned about tolerance when I was an undergrad at Whitman College. Like all good liberal arts colleges we freshmen were pulled aside and taught about tolerance. When I was a Junior, I even became a resident advisor and was trained to train other freshmen how to be tolerant. I remember one training session where we were dealing with a hypothetical. What if a foreign exchange student from South Africa put up their flag on the outside of their door? It was the end of the 1980s and apartheid was still practiced, so one by one my fellow tolerant classmates got up and explained how they would make this hypothetical student take down their flag. In an almost Southern Baptist-like church setting, each student had to "out politically correct" the previous student. It was kind of like who could yell "hallelujah" the loudest. So, by the end of the session on tolerance, I believe our mob-like consensus was summary execution for the student who had dared to put up a flag from their homeland.

That day still haunts me. I wish I had stood up. I wish I had said something. Don't get me wrong. You will never come across a more well-meaning group than my fellow resident advisors that day. They wanted to make the world a better place. But something had gone terribly wrong. In our lemmingesque (I don't care if it's a word or not … it's my book) pursuit of tolerance, we had become pseudo-fascists. I sat there that day thinking—would this guest to our country think we were so tolerant? But I was young. I didn't want to challenge the mob. I wasn't ready to be a heretic.

Not that I am against tolerance. All in all, I am a big fan of tolerance. I tend to come from the libertarian wing of the Republican Party, and if it were up to me, the government would spend less time telling people how to behave, no time telling people what to think, and I would add "live and let live" as the 28th Amendment to the Constitution. But, it turns out I don't have the authority to unilaterally add amendments to the Constitution, so I did something even more impractical. I tattooed my conservative credentials on my sleeve and went to graduate school.… in Eugene, Oregon!

I don't know if you have been to graduate school. If you have, you will know what I am talking about. If you haven't, let me explain it this way. If you want to save yourself four years of your life, and about $20,000 of debt but still want to know what it's like to be an out-of-the-closet conservative studying political science in a state-run graduate school in Eugene, Oregon, it's easy. Put this book down. Go outside and stand in your driveway. Then ask your friend to swing a 2x4 at your head as hard as humanly possible. That was my life. Everyday for four years. But if you really want the true flavor of it, as your friend is beating you to death with the 2x4, have him call you names. Fascist. Racist. Nazi.

Graduate students talk about dissent all the time. Dissent is the highest form of patriotism they are fond of quoting. Graduate students are never more at home or happier than when marching, burning, or chanting about something. When I was at Oregon someone from the Bush administration was coming to campus and a student who had drunk the Kool-Aid early and often at an east coast liberal arts college shouted, "We need to organize a protest." I asked, "What are we protesting?" Silly question. But the silence in the room was such that you would have thought I had passed out a deferential equation pop-quiz. Dissent for the sake of dissent was the order of the day.

But beneath the overt support for tolerating dissent, there exists on university campuses a suffocating homogeneity in terms of what type of dissent is acceptable. I have always joked that one could probably find more intellectual diversity at a Klan meeting than in a faculty meeting of any sociology department. Maybe a funny joke, but not a funny reality. On a university campus, comparing the President to Hitler is noble. Advocating for free trade in South America is capitalist oppression.... and heresy. I slowly began to learn the liberal code words that were hurled at conservative heretics that dared offer their own version of dissent. Opposition to slave reparations was racist. Who wants to be called a racist? In class or out. Opposition to late-term abortion was sexist. Who wants to be called a sexist? Especially if you're trying to find a date for Saturday night. If you supported free markets, you were a selfish elitist who hated poor people. If you advocated free trade, you were an imperialist. In general, support for limited government, judicial restraint, a credible military defense, individual responsibility, and free markets got you tagged with a whole host of ugly words. It was McCarthyism all over again. But this time, instead of wrapping themselves in the flag to justify their oppression, they wrapped themselves in the cloth of tolerance. They were their own judge, jury and executioner. They got to decide what was acceptable dissent, and what was not. Anything they disagreed with was labeled, ironically ... intolerance.

Out of the flames that were the continual barrage of name calling and the hypocrisy that was born of the intolerance of tolerance, the seeds of a heretic were being sown. I wasn't 19 years old this time. I did speak up. I dissented.

And I was labeled intolerant.

But for the grace of a few professors who took me under their wing, let me read Friedman and Hayek, and graded me on my work, not my opinions, I don't know where I would be today. I wish I could name them here. They have my eternal thanks. I was lucky. I often wonder how many of my brothers in spirit were not.

Now it was time to find a job. I was a newly minted Ph.D. with publications under my belt and a solid resume. My problem was that I hadn't published the "right type" of research. I wrote about the constitutionality of reparation packages and articles about tort reform. I didn't write papers with titles like *Deconstructing the Racist Imagery of Hallmark Cards*, *How the Phallic Structure of Bananas is Oppressive towards Women*, or *Free Markets and Genocide: Is there Really a Difference?* These are the papers you need to write in graduate school if you want offers from UC Berkeley, Brown, or Williams.

I did, however, get a few interview offers. And I knew that now was not the time to be brave, dissent, or be a heretic. Keep your head down and mouth shut was my approach. If they ask you about Reagan, just grunt disdainfully. I don't know if it was my good looks, the poor quality of other applicants, or a terrible mistake on the part of the hiring committee, but I did get a tenure track offer. And like any starving college student, I took it!

A lot of people, especially my liberal friends (yes, I have lots of them) ask me if academia is so hostile towards conservatives, why did you choose to become a professor? For the same reason you don't fight the war on terror in Nebraska. You have to go where the enemy is. If I was going to be a heretic, I was going to be a heretic where the heresy mattered. Otherwise, I would have just been a hermit. No one would care about Martin Luther if he had nailed his 95 Theses to a tree in the middle of the woods. This man had guts. He nailed them to the front door of the Catholic Church. That's my type of heretic. I could have retreated to the CATO Institute and been among friends, but you can't make many converts when you are preaching to the choir.

And I wanted to be there for students in a way that no one was there for me. Many conservative students go to college and are browbeat into submission. They have no outlet for their own view of the world. To twist a phrase of the left, I wanted to create an island of tolerance in a sea of hostility. But more importantly, I wanted to offer an alternative perspective to thousands of students who would most likely be spoon-fed one view of the world. Academia is supposed to be a "marketplace of ideas." The problem is that the market is a monopoly. Everyone reads Marx. No one reads Friedman. I didn't want to (and still don't) lead a crusade in my classroom. That would make me just as guilty as the people I am criticizing. But I did want to open student's eyes to respected scholars who had an alternative view of the world; people who saw the value in free markets, limited government, cultural assimilation, and a foreign policy based on something more than group hugs and passing out tofu. To this day, many students leave my class asking, "I am a senior. Why have I not been taught any of this stuff until now?" A fair question that should be directed at their deans, provosts, and boards of trustees. Maybe taxpayers who fund our public universities should start asking that question as well.

One answer to the question has been offered by David Brooks, a noted conservative columnist. He too feels that academia is far too one-sided and offered this explanation in the *Atlantic Monthly*:

> What we are looking at here is human nature. People want to be around others who are roughly like themselves. That's called community. It probably would be psychologically difficult for most Brown professors to share an office with someone who was pro-life, a member of the National Rifle Association, or an evangelical Christian. It's likely that hiring committees would subtly—even unconsciously—screen out any such people they encountered. Republicans and evangelical Christians have sensed that they are not welcome at places like Brown, so they don't even consider working there. <u>In fact, any registered Republican who contemplates a career in academia these days is both a hero and a fool.</u>

There is a lot of truth to what Brooks is saying. Academia is very homogeneous. Except for a few heretics like me, it is a liberal haven. For example, according to the Chronicle of Higher Education, "Of the more than $7-million that people in higher education have given to federal candidates and national political parties and committees for the 2008 elections, 76 percent has gone to Democrats." To be honest, I'm not sure if liberal academics are just richer than conservative academics, of if conservatives have to spend their money on body guards and fake IDs.

I digress. We were talking about how I got my first job in academia. It's pretty simple after the offer and acceptance. You live on Top Ramen for the three months between when you get your last graduate school stipend in June and your first paycheck in October. There is a difference, however, between what one worries about after landing a job in academia and getting one in the "real world." In the real world, you worry about finding your office, remembering the secretary's name, and hoping you will have enough work to do in the early days so that no one thinks it was a mistake to hire you. In academia that all takes a back seat to the one thing we all worry about—getting tenure.

Tenure, for those of you who don't know, is a status professors can achieve if they have published enough articles, taught enough classes, and earned enough grant money, to impress the already tenured professors at their college. When professors first arrive at a university, they have a probationary status. A new professor has to prove himself before the university will hire him on a permanent basis. The probationary period is usually about five or six years.

Technically speaking, tenure means you have "a legal right (property right) to your job." Once a professor gets tenure, it is almost impossible for the university to fire him. Tenure was originally developed to prevent administrators from firing professors who expressed political opinions at odds with their own. So, beyond the job security, tenure really means professors can say or write whatever they want (even if it is politically unpopular) without fear of getting fired. Ironically, tenure was originally conceived to protect liberal professors from their conservative administrator. Now, as the tables have turned, many conservative professors need tenure to protect themselves from their liberal colleagues.

For the first five or six years, tenure is the end-all, be-all of a professor's existence. Almost everything you do is decided by the question "Will this help me get tenure?" Should I write this article or that article? Should I agree to serve on this committee? Should I make friends with this person? Should I sell my SUV and buy a Prius ... just like the one the Department Chair owns? I'm not sure if there are any steadfast rules for getting tenure, but there are some definite rules about how NOT to get tenure. Here is a short list of things you should avoid when seeking tenure in a political science department:

- Putting a Bush/Cheney bumper sticker on your car
- Owning a car
- Agreeing to be the Faculty Advisor for the College Republicans
- Answering "Reagan" when a colleague asks you who the best president of the 20th Century was
- Eating meat
- Spelling women "w-o-m-e-n" instead of "w-o-m-y-n"
- All forms of country-western music
- Any admissions that you have seen or understand what a supply and demand curve is
- Talk about the latest episode of JAG or NCIS
- Church

- Being seen in the hall with someone who at some point in their life MAY have attended church

And above all else, when a local newspaper asks you to write a guest editorial, do not, I repeat, do NOT under any circumstances write that editorial about why you think President George W. Bush should be re-elected over Senator John Kerry. Among the many other things on the list above, this is where I failed. I didn't just fail. I failed on a magnitude so massive that it defies comprehension. Think of the guy who designed the Pinto … and then times that by 10. We are talking failure along the lines of "Don't worry about it Captain, it's just an iceberg."

It's that failure on my part which is the next part of the story.

2

Stepping Into The Firestorm

Before we get into examining my "big mistake," let's step back a bit. I have arrived at my new place of employ—Central Washington University. I am determined to be a good boy. Teach my classes well, publish impressive scholarly articles, and provide service to the university where it is needed. These are the things good assistant professors do to become more relaxed associate professors.

Things were unfolding according to plan. The student evaluations of my classes were high. I was publishing articles on direct democracy, tort reform, and voting behavior with impressive speed. So far, so good.

Then there was my first hiccup. In the summer before I got to CWU, I sent the department and the bookstore a list of books needed for the two classes I would teach in the fall: Constitutional Law and Introduction to American Government. The books had to be ordered before I arrived. I picked texts that gave the students a broad introduction to a variety of perspectives about law and politics. You know, "marketplace of ideas" type stuff. There was some very liberal stuff in there and some conservative stuff in there. Safe.

A few months after I arrived at the department, the department chair, who I had gotten to know quite well, and is still one of my favorite people in the world, pulled me into his office. He said he got a call "from an administrator" who was not happy about my book selections.

"Really. What did he say?" I asked.

"He asked me, 'what the hell is going on over there? Books by Scalia and Goldberg?'"

"Ahh." was my only response.

I knew exactly what he was talking about. In my Constitutional law class I had assigned several books, one of which was *A Matter of Interpretation* edited by Supreme Court Justice Antonin Scalia. It is the perfect book to introduce students to the competing theories of how the Constitution should be interpreted by judges. In the beginning, Justice Scalia sets out his way of interpreting the Constitution. But then he invites two of the legal world's most well-known liberals and vocal opponents of his ideas to attack his position. The responses are by Lawrence Tribe and Ronald Dworkin, two giants in the field of law who consistently argue for a liberal, loose, and expansive view of the Constitution. From an academic setting, it is the perfect book. Students get to see both sides of the issue and decide for themselves.

The other book was *Bias* by Bernard Goldberg. *Bias* is a book written by a 26-year veteran of CBS News that attacks the media for having a liberal bias. It is not an even book. It has an opinion and makes its case very well. So, in order to balance my class and ensure both perspectives, I added to the reading list a book by Noam Chomsky titled *Manufacturing Consent*. Chomsky is the ultimate liberal. He hates the United States and all it stands for. Plain and simple. But, he had written a book arguing that the media in America is biased to the right. So I assigned it to be fair. My students got an attack from the right and an attack from the left.

Didn't matter. "An administrator" was upset. They had seen the names Scalia and Goldberg at the bookstore. Someone was getting off the reservation. I didn't pull the books and I still assign them to this day. But it was a warning shot. We are watching. We know what you are doing. Be careful.

Advice, maybe, I should have taken. But I didn't. Just too much heretic in me I guess. So when the editor of the local paper called me, I probably should have said "no." I said "yes."

We have a local paper in town—the *Daily Record*. It's like any small town paper. A brief recap of the national news, some local human interest stories, and the what's going on about town section. My favorite part is the police blotter where they report things like "A woman called 911 to report a suspicious man walking his dog" and other dangerous things we need to know about. The other part I like is the editorial page. Almost every day, people with very little education, too much free time, and apparently an unhealthy mix of pharmaceutical drugs write letters to the editor. It's cheaper than the movies, but just as entertaining.

As part of the editorial page, the publishers invited four professors from up at the university, two liberals and two conservatives, to take turns each Wednesday to write about whatever political subject they would like. It's a great idea. It involves the university in the community, it's fair and balanced, and it evokes all kinds of responses from the readership. The round and round of the four professors they had chosen had been going on for years before I got there. But as luck would have it, one of the conservative professors had to beg off in the same year I arrived at CWU.

Now there are some things that are easy, and some things that are hard. Finding an apple in Wenatchee is easy. Finding a conservative at a university is hard. Finding a conservative who is willing to write a monthly column putting his conservative credentials on display for all his colleagues to see is damn near impossible. Unless you have someone like me working there.

So the call came in. Would I like to take over as a regular op-ed contributor to the *Daily Record*? Sure. What have I got to lose but my career and sanity?

I started writing once a month. Nothing really controversial. I took some shots at the Democratic Party, defended Bush, and generally advocated for free markets. It was kind of my coming out party, but like a party where your mom invited all the friends you don't like. There would be the occasional glare in the hallway, or I would walk around the corner and all of a sudden the conversation would stop. Hmmm. Wonder what they were talking about?

When I started writing, most of the debate was about the Iraq war, but by about nine months in, the debate started to turn towards the 2004 election. In October of 2004, a month before the election, I had written a column addressing a local issue that was resolved in the September primary. But, looking at a calendar one day, I realized that my turn to write again would not come around until mid-November and after the election. So, for the first time, I wrote two columns and decided I would wait until the last minute to decide which one to send in.

It is that second column that literally changed my life ... and I owe it all to my wife ... who hates politics at almost every level. The truth is, I almost didn't send in *the* column. The column that for a month made my name a household word on every political blog in the nation. It wasn't written in my typical style. It was more a soliloquy than an empirical argument. It was lofty, flowery, emotional but something I believed intensely. So like all good men in a quandary, I turned to my wife. I brought her copies of both columns, asked her to read them, and tell me which one was better.

She came back in less than ten minutes.

"This one."

Nothing else really. No explanation. Just

"This one."

She had handed me the second column.

When I look back on it, I realize how much a life can change by simple, almost meaningless acts that take place in a moment. This was one of them. Regardless of how my life turns out, in some ways it will turn out the way it does because my wife said

"This one."

Here is what I had written. I had titled it "The Choice of a Generation" but my editors changed the title to "Election Determines Fate of the Nation."

◆   ◆   ◆

"Election Determines Fate of the Nation"

No sarcasm in this column. No attempts at witty repartee. The topic is too serious and the stakes are too high. This November we will vote in the only election during our lifetime that will truly matter. Because America is at a once-in-a-generation crossroads, more than an election hangs in the balance. Down one path lies retreat, abdication, and a reign of ambivalence. Down the other lies a nation that is aware of it's past and accepts the daunting obligation its future demands. If we choose poorly, the consequences will echo through the next 50 years of history.

If we, in a spasm of frustration, turn out the current occupant of the White House, the message to the world and ourselves will be twofold. First, we will reject the notion that America can do big things. Once a nation that tamed a frontier, stood down the Nazis and stood upon the Moon, we will announce to the world that bringing democracy to the Middle East is too big a task for us. But more significantly, we will signal to future presidents that as voters, we are unwilling to tackle difficult challenges, preferring caution to boldness, embracing the mediocrity that has characterized other civilizations. The defeat of President Bush will send a chilling message to future presidents who may need to make difficult, yet unpopular decisions. America has always been a nation that rises to the demands of history regardless of the costs or appeal. If we turn away from that legacy, we turn away from who we are.

Second, we inform every terrorist organization on the globe that the lesson of Somalia was well learned. In Somalia we showed terrorists that you don't need to defeat America on the battlefield when you can defeat them in the newsroom. They learned that a wounded America can become a defeated America. 24-hour news stations and daily tracking polls will do the heavy lifting, turning a cut into a fatal blow. Except that Iraq is Somalia times ten. The election of John Kerry will serve notice to every terrorist in every cave that the soft underbelly of American power is the timidity of American voters. Terrorists will know that a steady stream of grisly photos for CNN is all you need to break the will of the American people. Our own self-doubt will take it from there. Bin Laden will recognize that he can topple any American administration without setting foot on the homeland.

It is said that America's WWII generation is its "greatest generation." But my greatest fear is that it will become known as America's "last generation." Born in the bleakness of the Great Depression and hardened in the fire of WWII, they may be the last American generation that understands the meaning of duty, honor, and sacrifice. It is difficult to admit, but I know these terms are spoken with only hollow detachment by many (but not all) in my generation. Too many citizens today mistake "living in America" as "being an American." But America has always been more of an idea than a place. When you sign on, you do more than buy real estate. You accept a set of values and responsibilities. This November, my generation, which has been absent too long, must grasp the obligation that comes with being an American, or fade into the oblivion they may deserve. I believe that 100 years from now, historians will look back at the election of 2004 and see it as the decisive election of our century. Depending on the outcome, they will describe it as the moment America joined the ranks of ordinary nations; or, they will describe it as the moment the prodigal sons and daughters of the greatest generation accepted their burden as caretakers of the City on the Hill.

◆   ◆   ◆

634 words. 634 words in a small town Eastern Washington newspaper with a circulation of about 5,000. On the day it came out, I read the paper just to make sure there weren't any typos, put it down, and never planned to think about it again. To be honest, I don't even have a copy of the original article. It went into the trash that night. And as I fully expected, nothing happened.

Until I got a single email on my office computer. It was from a man I did not know and who had no kids in my classes. He was writing to thank me for the editorial I had written in the Daily Record about a week ago. He told me he lived in Seattle, and hoped I would write more like it in the future.

From Seattle I thought. How did he get a copy of my article? As best I could figure, a student must have had a copy of the local paper in a car and had driven home for the weekend. Or, there was a "Parents' Day" on campus just a few days earlier. Some dad must have bought a local paper just to get the flavor of the town.

How wrong I was. Next day I came to work to find another email, but this one had been copied to the entire staff in the political science department. It was from an angry man also from Seattle. He opposed the war in Iraq, felt I was completely off base, pointed out that I had misspelled a word (he was right) and that I should issue an apology for writing the editorial.

Most of the staff just ignored the rant. But, it made me think. Two local papers found their way across the mountains to Seattle? Two dads had visited and bought a local paper? Was it just a coincidence? I had never received an email or call from anyone outside of Ellensburg about any editorial before this. Now I get two in two days?

It wasn't a coincidence. Next day … ten emails. Next day … fifty emails. And the numbers just kept getting bigger everyday. And from farther away. People from Oregon. Then Texas, and California, and New York. A week passes and I started getting emails from people in Europe. I got emails from Switzerland, Italy, Germany, and Iraq. What the heck was going on here? How did these people find me? How did they get a copy of my essay?

Luckily for me, I ran into my editor in the local grocery store. Good. I was going to get some answers.

"Mike, do you guys ever send out your stories or editorials over the A.P. wire or something like that?"

"Rarely. Sometimes we'll get a story that gets picked up."

"Did you send out my column from last Wednesday by any chance?"

"Nope."

End of discussion and no answers. But the next day, I get a phone call in my office. It is from a lady I know who is a local farmer. She is very excited.

"Matt. You're on the radio!"

"I'm on the radio? I'm right here in my office."

"Kirby Wilbur is reading your essay on the air right now!"

"Who is Kirby Wilbur?" I asked, not knowing at the time that Kirby has one of the largest radio audiences in Seattle.

"He is a Seattle talk-show host. He is reading your essay right now. You should try and go find a radio!"

Well, I didn't have a radio. So I went back to work. But now, my interest was peaked. I wanted to know what was going on and how it got started. I went back to the first guy who sent me an email. Maybe that was the beginning. I wrote him an email asking where he had got a copy of my article. He told me he was a Vietnam veteran and had seen it posted on a Vietnam veteran website. To this day I don't know who did it, but apparently, someone took the time to sit down and re-type my essay. I know it didn't come from the newspaper. They don't post their editorial section online. I know I didn't send out any email copies. Someone felt strong enough to re-type my essay and post it on a website.

From there it had entered the digital world. Anyone could "cut and paste" it into an email or re-post it on a blog. It turns out, much to my surprise, that everyone is on someone's email list. It only takes days for the web of interconnected family and friends email lists to span the globe. It can even come full circle back to Ellensburg. A student walked into my class and announced,

"My aunt sent me an essay to read and you wrote it."

"Really. Where does your aunt live?

"Italy."

It really has become a small world. And a crowded one at that. I got a call back from my editor. Same guy I had talked to in the store a few days earlier.

"Matt. Is there something going on with your editorial?"

"Yes. I'm getting emails about it from all over the world. That's why I asked you about the A.P. in the store the other day. Why? What's going on over at the Record?"

"Well, we usually get about 1000 or so hits on our website each month. We're getting about 4,000 hits a day. We're also fielding phone calls asking for copies of your article. We don't usually do this, but were going to post it on the website."

I was getting an education in how the new age media are all connected. I had never read a "blog" in my life up to this point. But, as was news to me at the time, there are people called "bloggers" who spend a lot of time surfing the web, reading news articles and editorials, and then post them on their blogs. They usually make a comment or two and then allow other readers—people who have visited their blog—to make comments.

It seems there is a "pecking order" to these blogs. Some are more prestigious than others and it's usually readership numbers, or what they call "hits," that determines status. A big name blog can get millions of hits in a year. My essay got picked up by a blog called *The Free Republic*. It's a big one apparently.

I was also starting to attract the wrath of liberal bloggers. If there is a bible of blogs for the Left it is a blog called the *Daily Kos*. It is fair to say these people hate me. They are not particularly bright folks and seem to only know adjectives that are spelled with four letters, but I became enemy number one for a day or two. Apparently, they don't have much of an attention span either. I got called all types of names. The only ones I can print here are "chicken-hawk" and "wing-nut". But I had been called worse.

What I didn't realize at the time was that talk radio show hosts have a lot of time to fill. Some are on the air for three hours every day. I complain about hour and a half lectures. Not any more. To find things to talk about, they read newspapers, read blogs, and get emails from their listeners. A lot of radio show hosts got emails with my essay in it. Kirby Wilbur out of Seattle, Washington was the first. More were to follow.

About two weeks or so into this maelstrom that had become my life, I get a call from a woman named Laura Ingraham. It's embarrassing to admit, but at the time, I had no idea who she was. And she could tell.

"You don't know who I am do you?" She asked me.

"Well, I teach all day. I don't really listen to talk radio." I replied. It's true. I have heard about five Rush Limbaugh shows in my entire life. It's usually as I am driving through Nevada.

"Well, you should." She told me.

Turns out Ms. Ingraham is the real deal. She is a regular on Fox News and has her own syndicated show out of New York. She also has lots of listeners. I can tell you that I tried to respond to EVERY email, pro or con that someone sent me. But after her show, it became impossible. Just too many. And I did have a day job teaching students and responding to their emails.

It also turns out that once you have been on the Ingraham show, every other radio talk show host wants you on their show too. Now the maelstrom had changed. Instead of just getting hundreds of emails a day, I was also getting phone calls from all over the country to be on talk radio shows. Too damn many of them on the east coast. "Drive time" is big a deal for these guys and since it is three hours earlier out there, I found myself getting up at 4:30 am each day to do a series of call-in shows. I was glad to do it. I believed in what I had written and it seemed to be having a real effect on the election. Most political scientists go their entire lives and never affect the elections we study. I was making a difference. Many of the emails I got were from people on the fence. A lot told me, "I was undecided until I read your article, but now I'm voting for Bush." I was young, having an impact, and getting up at 4:30 a.m. to keep the ball rolling. For the record, my wife was NOT a big fan of the 4:30 a.m. thing. Go figure.

Eventually, I had to get strategic. Too many radio stations, not enough time in the day. So I started taking interviews only in swing states. Anyone who asked from Ohio, Missouri, and Florida got an automatic yes. Radio stations in dark blue states started to get a no. And radio stations in solid red states got a maybe. Let me tell you something. Ohio has way too many radio stations!

Obviously, as the dissemination got wider, the ratio of positive and negative emails started to even out. When the hub-bub got started, people of like minds were mailing it to each other, so the comments were mostly positive. But, we were an evenly divided nation in 2004. Bush only won with 51% of the vote. It was only a matter of time before my essay started to get read by other academics. To put it mildly, they were not pleased. I started receiving emails from academics at universities all over the United States, about 99% of them negative. The attacks generally fit into three groups. 1) You come from a small school so your opinions don't matter. 2) You will never get tenure. 3) You have betrayed your profession.

"You come from a small school that no one has heard of." "Who gives a damn what you think." "If you had any credibility, you would have been hired by a better university." That was the gist of many of the emails in the first category. One thing people need to understand is that there is a fundamentally different culture in universities on the East Cost than on the West Coast. Out West professors don't demand that you call them "doctor," we don't call each other "professor" unless it's a formal occasion, we dress down a little and there is relatively little pedigree boasting. That type of stuff is more prevalent in East Coast colleges. So, when I started getting nasty emails from "colleagues" from the Ivy League, there were a lot of cheap shots about my school, where I went to graduate school, and why that made me a joke.

Here is something I found very interesting. The blue collar workers who disagreed with me wrote more eloquent and mature responses than did my fellow academics. The "average Joe," if there is such a thing, would respond by simply pointing out the areas on which they disagreed, highlight some evidence that supported their views, and then sign off. Many of the replies from academics were petulant, nasty, and resembled something you would hear on a junior high playground. I found that strange then and I still find it strange today.

The second thread of attacks was about tenure. Often, they were very short. I remember getting one email that simply read,

"Good luck with tenure buddy."

These types of comments were the only ones that made me really angry. I don't care if people want to attack my school. I know it's a good school. Additionally, I don't care if people want to attack me. I put myself and my views out there. I had to expect return fire. That's just part of the game we play. But for a fellow academic to make a comment about me getting tenure because I had publically expressed support for the President was simply chilling. It suggested that there were academics in the social sciences that voted for tenure based on the political views of the professor rather than the quality of their scholarship and teaching. No wonder most of our universities lean to the left, I thought. If you have to pass a thought police screening test to earn it, of course we are going to end up with a very homogeneous environment.

I have not gone up for tenure yet, and based on the people I know at Central, my political views will not be held against me. But others have not been so lucky. Renowned academic Mike Adams, who teaches at University of North Carolina—Wilmington was denied promotion because he wrote a weekly column for the National Review, a noted conservative publication. Here is what the American Defense Fund, the legal group defending professor Adams, wrote about the controversy,

> Adams, hired to teach at UNCW in 1993, and an associate professor since 1998, generated an impressive record of productive research resulting in 10 peer-reviewed publications, the number UNCW department chairs had stated as "safe" to merit promotion to full professor. Adams applied for full professorship in 2004, but the then-interim chair of the department, Dr. Diane Levy, known as an outspoken feminist with leftist political leanings, raised concerns about Adams' "political activity" and reprimanded him for his weekly nationally syndicated column. Contrasting him with columnist William F. Buckley, Levy requested that Adams change his writing style so that it would be less "caustic" and more "cerebral."

> In 2005, Dr. Kimberly J. Cook became chair of the Department of Sociology and Criminal Justice at UNCW. Cook, an outspoken atheist who openly criticized Christianity, described to a recruitment committee her ideal candidate for a teaching position as "a lesbian with spiked hair and a dog collar." Adams completed his 11th peer-reviewed publication in 2006 and applied for promotion to full professorship. But during a closed-door meeting on Sept. 14, Cook and senior faculty members decided not to promote Adams.

So much for the "market place of ideas." When I think about how many academics jumped to the defense of Ward Churchill, the offensive bigot from the University of Colorado who called the victims of the World Trade Center "little Eichmanns" and their deaths as "justice," but who turned on and ousted Harvard President Larry Summers over comments about gender and math skills, I am reminded of the hypocrisy in my field that sometimes rears its ugly head. Dang. That was a long sentence.

The third type of criticism I got from my fellow academics was that somehow I had "betrayed my profession." Obviously, I didn't get the memo that said all academics have to follow the liberal line, but I received multiple reminders after my essay hit the airways. Many of the email responses just expressed incredulity. HOW COULD YOU?! An academic of all people. All I can say is that they must not have got my memo. There is a heretic in your midst. And a vocal one at that.

Beyond all the criticism and congratulations, there was one event that was bound to put this controversy behind me—Election Day. That day came, and to my great relief, President Bush was re-elected. Coincidentally, I was slated to publish my regular Wednesday column the day after Tuesday night's election. But my column had to be to the editors that Monday. So there I was, sitting in front of my computer, staring at a blank screen, and knowing that I had to write my column before election night, but that it would not be published until after election night.

If you remember, the polls taken just before the election had the race neck-and-neck. Mr. Zogby, a prominent national pollster, had even predicted a Kerry victory on election eve. What was I going to write about? I couldn't write about a Bush or Kerry victory, people were sick of political analysis, and a prediction about the election results would be silly. I ended up writing a column about the story I have just related. People knew that my column had gone world-wide, but most people didn't know the details. And I needed catharsis. Writing the column "Election Night" helped me find it.

◆   ◆   ◆

"Election Night"

Due to a quirk in scheduling, this column had to be written before the election but will not be published until after. Therefore, as I write, I have no idea who will be the next president of the United States and see no need to make politics the focus of this week's column.

As most of you already know, the column that I wrote last month got picked up by e-mail lists, bloggers, news radio talk show hosts, and a variety of other media. The resulting exposure led to 1000s of e-mail responses, 100s of phone calls, and several national media interviews. I got my Andy Warhol anointed "15 minutes of fame." I'm looking forward to returning to the obscurity most academics enjoy. I'm sure that most of the people who objected to the content of the essay are hoping the same thing.

But the experience has taught me many things. I encounter truisms such as "the world is getting smaller" all the time. But it's not until you start getting e-mails from people in Germany responding to an essay you wrote in Ellensburg, that this starts to hit home. The notion that there is only "six degrees of separation" between all people on the Earth also has more meaning to me now. I have received emails from ex-college friends and ex-students from around the United States looking me up to let me know they received a copy of my article.

I have also been reminded that words still count. I am completely astounded by the passion my 634 words evoked. I have messages from people who told me they wept after reading the article. And, despite the fact I did not use any derogatory language (no one was called a fascist, idiot, or even a flip-flopper) I have emails from people who read the same article telling me they hate me with all of the intensity they can muster. It reminds me that the study of America can some-times be covered by studying the rhetoric of America. Do we study Washington, Lincoln, and Roosevelt, or do we study the "Farewell Address", the "Gettysburg Address" and "Fireside Chats"? Not that I compare myself to these men in any way (please no more emails), but I am reminded of the profound truth that sometimes ideas are more powerful than armies.

The experience also leads me to thank several people who were, through no actions of their own, caught up in the whirlwind that has been the past few weeks. I would like to thank Mike Gallagher and Tim Engstrom, editors of *The Daily Record*. They were inundated with requests for reprints, queries about the authenticity of the article, and demands for copies. As far as I know, they turned no one away.

I would also like to think Professor Jim Brown, my department chair. Most people probably think that Jim and I, because of our different political opinions, engage in daily sword duels in the hallway. It is simply not true (we use light sabers). Professor Brown was also deluged with e-mails and phone calls (angry and supportive). While some citizens felt that I should not be allowed to place my title and institutional affiliation next to my column, Jim, and others in the department, defended my right to do so.

I know I said I would avoid politics in this column, but I offer this last thought (so I'm a flip flopper). The recent presidential election has been intense and passionate. The rhetoric has been fervent. As I sit here, I don't know who won. But regardless of who won, I hope we can take the next few months to pull back a little and treat the winner with the respect he deserves.

◆   ◆   ◆

I think the country was exhausted after the 2004 elections. I know I was. There was an intensity that we don't always see in American politics. More money, more vitriol, more participation. But like all things, that intensity has to ebb lest it consume us whole. The election was over and so was my Andy Warhol "fifteen minutes of fame." Sort of. The radio show spots stopped immediately. The emails started to abate after the election with just an occasional "thank you" email. But my name was out there and Google has basically immortalized those fifteen minutes for anyone who wants to search "Manweller."

To this day, however, I still run into people who ask me "about that guy from Central who wrote that Bush essay." In my current life, I spend a lot of time touring the state speaking at conventions, association meetings, and political events. When being introduced, the host typically notes that I am a political scientist who teaches at Central. Without exception, I get someone after my speech come up to me and ask if I know that guy who wrote "the essay" back in 2004.

"You mean that really good looking guy?" I usually respond to blank stares.

3

Out Of The Firestorm, Into The Fire

Once you have had your name and picture spread all over the Internet, anonymity is a thing of the past. I now lived in world where after I said, "Hi, I'm Professor Manweller" I had to hold my breath for just a moment to see if there was going to be a hug or a confrontation.

As is the tradition at Central, many professors come out on the first day of school and help new freshman move in. It's a day of menial labor toting lava lamps and stereos bigger than my first car up the stairs. I go to help, but also to remind myself why I spent so many years in school. During the first Fall after my big Bush article, I'm standing outside the dorms helping parents part with their kids and more importantly, their kid's junk, when a nice family pulls up in their car. We start unloading suitcases and such and make a trip up the stairs. Eventually I introduce myself and the father knows who I am. He's read the article, spread the article, and I suspect made his son read the article. At this point, I am no longer allowed to help carry his son's stuff. Instead, we end up having a twenty minute conversation about politics outside the dorm. At this point, I start to realize that my life is probably not going to completely return to "normal" anytime soon. (As a side note, I am still friends with the family I met that day.)

If you are smart, you can get your anonymity back if you keep quite and don't volunteer for anything. I wasn't that smart. Instead of slinking back to my office and quietly publishing more exciting articles on obscure Supreme Court cases from the 1800s, I started compiling another list of things NOT to do if you want your anonymity back. The list goes something like this:

- Do not get elected Chairman of the Republican Party.
- Do not start your own conservative radio talk show.

- Do not become the producer and host of a political television show.

- Do not agree to debate Robert Kennedy Jr. in a hotel lobby with a Time magazine reporter as moderator.

- Do not show up on television so often that the Democratic Party starts following you around with a television camera of their own.

I, not being that smart, ended up doing all of the things on that list. Before I tell you about them, I should probably add one more item to the list. If you do all those things, you should not sit down and write a book about it, reminding everyone that you did those things. But if you ignore this sound advice, don't title your book *The Right Opinion: A Heretic's Voice from the Ivory Tower*. Not because it's a bad name, but because it's taken and I don't want the competition.

When I was a kid, my grandfather used to ask me a simple riddle. "How far can a dog run into the forest?" The answer is "halfway." As soon as he gets halfway in, my grandfather would say, he is then running out of the forest. I didn't really get it when I was younger, but I was starting to see the wisdom of the riddle as I sat there with a gavel in my hand as the newly elected Chairman of the Kittitas County Republican Party. What the hell, I was already half way in; I might as well keep running. According to my grandfather, if I kept going, I would be heading out.

Here is a promise I can make you. You can count on one hand the number of Republican Party chairmen who are professors at universities. For starters, being a Republican on a university campus is a lot like having lice. It's socially icky, and you definitely don't go around telling people about it. Luckily for these few Republican professors, voting takes place in the privacy of a booth or their home. They don't have to let anyone know. That is unless you go and get yourself elected as the Chairman of the Republican Party. Then, it's a little harder to "stay in the closet." Being handed that gavel was a lot like getting "outed."

If you think I am exaggerating, let me relate to you a tale about a friend of mine who is also a Republican and a professor, but teaches at a much larger and far more liberal university. He and I were both invited to speak to the University of Washington's College Republicans about voting trends in Washington State. It was a pretty straight forward event. Thirty or so students in room. Two speeches. Two question and answer periods. All is done and we are headed for a beer. But then my friend realizes he has left some handouts in the room. Not originals or anything, just some photocopies.

"We have to go back" he says.

"Really?" I respond. "Are they your only copies?"

"No. I just don't want anyone to find them."

"WHO to find them?" I ask.

"Another professor" he replies.

It turns out my friend was nervous about the possibility that another professor would come in, see the documents and figure out that he had spoken to the College Republicans. I thought he might be joking, but he was serious. Just the knowledge that he had *spoken* to the College Republicans might jeopardize his promotion. "Wow" I remember thinking to myself. If just speaking to a Republican student group can get you in trouble, I wonder what getting elected as Chair of the Party gets you into?

Before I could answer that question, I found another way to get myself into trouble. One day, I'm having a cup of coffee and Bob, a friend of mine, calls me and says, "We ought to start a radio show ... a political talk show like Rush Limbaugh." Ya Bob, I'm sure if we just walk into the radio station, tell them we have absolutely no on-air experience, they'll just hand us our own radio show.

That's pretty much what happened. Bob called a local radio station and set up a lunch meeting with the news producer. At the meeting, Bob and I got into a political argument about doctor-assisted suicide which captivated the attention of the producer, the waitress, and all the tables within a napkin throwing distance. That was enough for the producer. We were on the air the next week.

So, at this point, you can see that I am NOT doing a very good job developing a lower profile. I'm writing a conservative op-ed piece for the local paper every month, I'm on the air railing against liberals and Democrats every Friday on the local radio station, and I am serving as the local chairman of the Republican Party. This is a game plan only Jack Kevorkian would like. On the up side, it appears there is no way I can get more media attention than I already have.

I was wrong.

Once again I made the mistake of answering my phone when it rang. I have to stop doing that. This time the other end of the phone was held by a local television producer who wanted to create a political talk show akin to *Face the Nation* or *Meet the Press*. He wanted my ideas about how the show should be formatted, what topics might be interesting, and who I thought might be a good host and producer for the show.

I took some time to scribble out about ten episode topics, craft some suggestions for format, and even gave him some names of people to host the show. My work here was done. Except that I got another phone call a few weeks later.

"You seem to have a pretty good grasp of this material and some really good ideas for format ... would you be interested in being the host?"

"NO" is such a simple word. I'm pretty good at telling my students "no." I am great at telling telemarketers "no." I am not good at saying "no" to my wife when she wants new shoes or when someone asks me to volunteer for something political. The first is going to catch up to my Visa bill, the other is going to catch up to my sanity. Regardless, as you can probably already imagine, I did not say "no."

Thus, the monthly political talk show known as "Point to Point" was born. Now, if the weekly radio show, monthly newspaper column, and Republican chairmanship weren't enough, people could see my face on TV every week. I should point out, as my wife is apt to do from time to time, that I don't get paid for any of these activities. I believe this fact was one of the reasons my wife told me, "Why don't you write a book. You can at least sell that."

When Andy Warhol said that in the future everyone would get fifteen minutes of fame, he forgot to mention that the first fifteen minutes can be just the first domino rattling into others. Without any intention, and almost no effort, I had stumbled upon notoriety. If I had known this was coming, I would have tried to be better looking.

Notoriety is a double-edged sword. It brings some interesting moments, but also some unwanted attention. On the interesting side, every once in a while my wife and I end up at parties we have no business being at. For example, we got invited to a huge political event some time back. When we arrived, Attorney General Rob McKenna and his wife were sitting to our left and Dino Rossi and his wife were sitting to our right. We had only one question. What the hell were we doing there?

On the down side, notoriety also attracts the attention of the "crazies". I am not sure there should be quotes around the word crazies, but I leave it in to avoid lawsuits. As just one example, there is a man in town who is regularly in and out of jail, but whenever he is out of jail writes lengthy emails to everyone in town blaming me, the President of CWU, and the local prosecuting attorney of conspiring to keep him in jail. I don't know why he picked us three. I especially don't know why he picked me. But I am learning there is a price to pay for losing your anonymity.

And then sometimes, notoriety brings you something that is neither good nor bad, but just bizarre. In my case, as is typical, it starts with a phone call.

"Hello. Is Professor Manweller there?"

"Yes. Speaking."

"My name is xxxx and I am a reporter with Time Magazine."

"THE Time Magazine."

"Yes."

"What can I do for you?"

"Well, as you know, Robert Kennedy Jr. is in town tonight to discuss the environment and the Bush Administration. I am interested in getting some quotes from some people who hold different views. Would you be willing to meet with me after his speech?"

I agreed to meet with the reporter after the speech. The speech by the way, was a two hour screed about how Bush was the Devil incarnate and that the end of the world was near if the President did not leave office immediately. My favorite part was when he was blasting the media for being irresponsible and complacent in promoting Bush, and then telling people he got his news from Al Franken on Air America. You want quotes Mr. Time Magazine guy; I got some quotes for you.

My "meeting" with Mr. Time Magazine did not go as I had anticipated. When I walked into the hotel at which he was staying, I was met in the lobby by Mr. Kennedy himself. The reporter says,

"Instead of me asking you some questions, I thought the two of you could just debate and I would take notes."

So there began one of the more surreal moments of my life. It was about 11:30 p.m. and I was standing in the lobby of a Holiday Inn Express debating environmental policy with the son of Robert Kennedy. This is not something I had envisioned happening in my life. Ever. But debate we did. He argued for government. I argued for markets. He argued for laws and penalties. I argued for incentives and rewards. Round and round. It was fun. About 30 minutes later, we shook hands and he went to bed. I don't think I changed his mind a bit, and likewise in the other direction. But at least now, when I am very old, I can start sentences with "When I was debating Robert Kennedy...." and my grandchildren will roll their eyes.

Falling into the category of weird more than bizarre is when I found out that the Democratic Party had ordered an intern to follow me around with a camera at my public events. I'm not quite sure how I became such a threat to the Washington State Democratic Party that they felt the need to record my every move, but apparently, heretics in the ivory tower scare them. I don't hold any political power, I am not an elected official of any kind, but for some reason, an educated man who speaks about the value of limited government, the effectiveness of free markets and free trade, and the necessity of individual responsibility needs to be monitored with video cameras by the Democratic Party. I never realized ideas scared them so badly. It must be why they don't have any.

The first time I realized they were filming me was when I was speaking at the Slade Gorton Lecture Series hosted by the Discovery Institute in Seattle, Washington. I had been invited to speak about the same topic as this book: liberalism and academia. When I showed up, there were three TV cameras in the back of the room. When my speech was over, I asked the staff who the three cameras were for. One was for TVW, the statewide public television station in Washington, the second was for the Discovery Institute since they keep records of all their events, and the last one was for the Democratic Party. If only I had known, I would have waived and said "Hi" to Mrs. Gregoire and State Chairman Dwight Pelz. I would have also asked them a question. Who sends a cameraman to record an event that is going to BE ON TV?! Is it any wonder these people run up huge deficits? They could have saved a few bucks and just watched it ... ON TV.

The last story I have to pass on is about how I got ambushed by two students at a First Amendment Festival. The festival was designed to educate students about the different parts of the First Amendment and then impress upon them the importance of the Amendment in our daily lives. I was a member of the "steering committee" and helped put together many of the events. The events were varied and sometimes controversial. We wanted to be controversial … why else would you have a First Amendment Festival. We had the head of the national ACLU come speak. Gloria Steinem, a leading liberal feminist came. The past head of the Black Panthers came. We held "Banned Books" events, banned art exhibits, and more. We even had a past Seattle cop come and talk about the need to legalize all drugs. This was not a "conservative" festival by any means.

So what lead to me getting waylaid by two angry young liberal students? Tim Eyman, the noted anti-tax crusader was invited by yours truly to attend a panel on direct democracy. One of our First Amendment panels was created to educate students about the initiative process and Tim being the most well-know initiative activist in the state was a big catch for us. At the end of the panel, two students came right up to me and said they were huge supporters of the First Amendment Festival but demanded that people like "him" be banned from speaking at the festival or any other event on campus.

"Let me get this straight. You love the First Amendment Festival, but you want someone banned from speaking at it?" I asked.

"Yes. He is anti-human rights. He should not be allowed to speak" was the response.

"Do you understand what the First Amendment Festival is about?" I questioned.

"It's about freedom and he is against freedom. He should not be allowed on campus."

At this point, the head of the entire festival, who is a proud liberal herself, was listening to the conversation. You could see the look of disappointment in her eyes. She had spent months creating a festival that would promote freedom, tolerance, and free expression and here were two students that completely failed to grasp their own hypocrisy. They were demanding censorship at a First Amendment celebration! ACLU advocates calling for the impeachment of President Bush were okay. Black Panthers calling for violence were okay. A cop demanding the legalization of drugs was fine. But a man calling for lower taxes? He should be banned as anti-human rights.

I think that story, as much as any other, exemplifies the contradictions that continues to exist on college campuses everywhere. These two students were well-meaning kids. They passionately believed what they were doing was right. But, having spent four years in such a homogeneous environment, they had lost the ability to see their own contradictions. Their demand for "tolerance" had become fascist—and they couldn't even see it.

Whenever the alarm clock goes off too early and I just don't have the energy to walk into the classroom, I try to remember those two students. It reminds me of why I need to be in the classroom. Real tolerance comes with real education. Real education can only be accomplished if students are introduced to all ideas, not just those ideas that pass the "politically correct" test.

If that memory doesn't get me going in the morning, all I have to do is get off the elevator to my office and walk to the billboard that is up for the College Democrats and College Republicans to post announcements. On the College Republican side is a poster. The poster announces meeting times and contact information. The poster has been defaced by a student who has scribbled "AKA Nazi Youth" through the middle of it. It reminds me I have lots of work still to do.

Much of that work involves writing columns, op-ed pieces, and policy briefs in an attempt to educate citizens about the value of limited government. The rest of this book is the "ideas" part of the book. As I said earlier—my ideas. I address all types of topics, but I have categorized them into sections which include my thoughts on: Democrats, Republicans, Europeans, Public Policy, the War on Terror, and Free Markets and Free Trade.

4

Democrats

"Mad Cows and Mad Democrats" was the first column I ever wrote for my local paper. At the time, the U.S. was experiencing its first ever case of mad cow disease. It was a serious issue in Eastern Washington where cattle was, and still is, big business. I remember gubernatorial candidate Dino Rossi came to Mabton, Washington right after the news broke. Mabton is a small town on the I-82 with a big beef industry and they were understandably nervous. Dino got up and gave a short speech. He said something to the effect of "I had a hamburger for breakfast, I had a hamburger for lunch, and I'm having a steak for dinner." The crowd went wild.

At the same time, national Democrats were getting over their post September 11th "We're all in this together" feelings. The attacks on President Bush were getting ugly. It was still early in the campaign and the smart money was still on Howard Dean. I remember looking at a newspaper headline about mad cow disease then thinking those cows aren't half as mad as these Democrats are. Thus, my first column was born.

◆   ◆   ◆

"Mad Cows and Mad Democrats"

America currently confronts two problems: mad cows and mad Democrats. Whereas the cows are neither angry nor insane, Democrats around the country appear to be both. If I were a Democrat looking at my presidential candidates, I'd be insanely angry myself. But that's a column for a different day. Democrats are angry because President Bush is turning out to be right. And nothing upsets Democrats more than when people who wear cowboy hats and hail from Texas are right about anything—even if it's the weather.

For the past two years Democrats have taken every opportunity to assail the current administration over its assertive foreign policy. At home, President Bush has been called "stupid" and "dangerous." Meanwhile, most of our European "allies" are hoping that Neville Chamberlain will be selected as the Democratic nominee; the ostrich approach to foreign policy worked so well for them in the past, they want to give it one more try. What makes Liberals and Europeans so ineffectual is their unwavering belief in moral relativism. To them, Saddam Hussein is not "wrong" he is simply "different." Therefore, they are uncomfortable with any foreign policy based on the notions of right and wrong.

But something funny happened on the way to Baghdad: Bush's foreign policy started paying dividends. Syria, long a state sponsor of terrorism, has become more cooperative in the past few months. Iran signed on to the nuclear proliferation accords. And the biggest coup, Libya, long a state sponsor of terrorism, abandoned its weapons of mass destruction programs.

Of course, we could assume this had nothing to do with the tough stance of the President. Maybe the Syrians truly want peace in the Middle East and their funding of Hamas was carried out by renegade bureaucrats. Maybe Kadaffi realized his true purpose in the world was to bring safety and harmony to his fellow man. Maybe the Ayatollahs are a misunderstood cabal who want to live peacefully with the West. Maybe tomorrow I will wake up, look like Tom Cruise, and Brittney Spears will stop by with a pizza. Hey, as long as were in fantasy land....

The reality of foreign policy is that it is not essential to be popular and well-liked. It is essential to be respected and sometimes even feared. It's not about having "group hugs" with the family of nations but ensuring that when you speak, your words have meaning. When Mr. Clinton spoke, many liked what they heard, but all would question whether he really meant it. When Mr. Bush speaks, no one doubts he means what he says; nor that he will back it up with action. When Bush says he will follow a policy of preemption, the Middle East acts because they know he means it. When Democrats talk about foreign policy, the Middle East acts when the French sign off on it.

Walter Lippmann once observed that the difficulty democracies have with foreign policy is that idealistic rhetoric is more appealing than hard choices. There is a strong idealistic current in American culture. We are attracted to leaders who claim that peace and security can be achieved with tolerance, compassion, and a willingness to compromise. But these characteristics require a two-way street. As long as many in the Arab world despise America because we ensure women's rights, value religious tolerance, and follow a Constitution rather than a holy book, they will be unwilling to offer tolerance, compassion, and compromise to us. If John "I voted for the war but refused to fund it" Kerry or any other Democrat thinks he will be able to protect America by making nice with the enemy, delegating national security to the UN, and coddling the French, no one around here is going to be safe.

◆   ◆   ◆

Looking back at your own writing is always hard. You have to admit mistakes. Some of your predictions turn out wrong. I still feel Bush does not get enough credit for pushing the Libyans away from terrorism. In hindsight, however, the Iranians and the Syrians didn't come around as much as I had hoped. For a while the Lebanese looked as if they might demand independence from Hamas and Syrian interference, but it turned out to be a revolution that wasn't.

Being an election year, 2004 provided ample opportunity for me to criticize Democratic policies and candidates. In some ways, I did it on purpose. I wanted the readership to know what they were in for. As a result, I think my first few columns caught a lot of people by surprise. "Conservative professor" just doesn't roll off the tongue and people don't expect it. I went to a local meeting and a legislator was on the panel. When I asked a question, he actually recognized me. "Hey, you are that professor from Central." I wasn't used to being recognized by anyone but students. But being a conservative professor made me a novelty of some sort.

One of the things that really made me angry during the early part of the Iraq war was how Democrats could dish out the criticism, but couldn't take any themselves. When they were criticizing the war effort, it was "dissent is patriotic … the good citizen criticized their government." But, if anyone criticized Democrats in turn, those people were "stifling dissent." I saw it as hypocrisy and said so in "The Curse of Sporadic Patriotism."

◆   ◆   ◆

"The Curse of Sporadic Patriotism"

The Iraq war has been the source of intense partisan debate. Criticisms have been levied by both parties about each other's respective approaches to foreign policy. As part of this debate, some Democrats have protested that they are being unjustly labeled as "unpatriotic." They assert that the true patriot challenges their government; points out when the government is wrong. I agree with the central tenants of their argument. It was the Democratic Senator William Fulbright who epitomized the ideal of "critic as patriot" during the Vietnam War. I also agree that the 1st Amendment should never be sacrificed in times of war. However, to borrow a line from Shakespeare: "Me thinks the lady doth protest too much."

The problem is that some Democrats think that they get to criticize the President, and then hide behind the shield of patriotism to avoid being criticized in return. I call it "sniper patriotism." You hop up, take a pot shot at the President, and then hide behind the shield of free speech and patriotism. If anyone returns fire, they are impugning your patriotism. How convenient. If Democrats are going to be "patriotic" and criticize the President, then expect Republicans to be equally "patriotic" and respond with fervor. It is interesting that when Democrats levy vitriolic and personal criticisms towards President Bush they are simply being patriotic. But when Republicans criticize Democrats, they are extremists "playing the patriotism card."

What I also find so interesting is the schizophrenic nature of Democratic patriotism. Where was this "patriotism" during the Kosovo war? Did the Green Party march on Olympia demanding a resolution to end hostilities? Where were all the ex-hippies with their tie-dye shirts and Grateful Dead albums marching in the street? Where were all those liberal college students conducting "peace-ins" during that conflict? Could they not find their "patriotism" back then? Could it possibly be that some Democrats tend to be more "patriotic" when there is a Republican president? No. That would be too cynical. Manipulating patriotism for political purposes? Not our party!

The thing is, I believe President Clinton was correct to engage in the Kosovo conflict just as I believe that President Bush is correct in Iraq. I don't think there should have been protests in the street. Does that make me less patriotic?

I can already anticipate the response to this column. It will go like this. Iraq is completely different than Kosovo. But is it really? The criticisms of the Iraq war are generally threefold. Hussein was not a direct threat. We ignored the international community by not utilizing the UN. We should have allowed more time for inspections to work. But let's look at the Kosovo war. Was Slobodan Milosevic a direct threat to the US? Surely not. America was never threatened by that brutal dictator. Furthermore, Clinton did a complete end run around the UN because Russia and China, both members of the Security Council, promised vetoes of any UN action. He had to come up with his own "coalition of the willing." And, could we have not used economic sanctions to bring the Milosevic regime to its knees?

The only real difference between Iraq and Kosovo is that in the first conflict we had a Democratic president and in the latter conflict we had a Republican president. What a testament to Bush's leadership skills. He is able to tap into Democratic "patriotism" when presidents from their own party couldn't (yes, that was sarcasm). Democrats want to criticize President Bush and then insulate themselves from a response by hiding behind the shield of patriotism. It doesn't work that way. The *credible* patriot both supports and criticizes his country *regardless* of which party is in power.

◆   ◆   ◆

Another thing I often took Democrats to task for was their tendency to exaggerate everything. Their hyperbole sometimes approached the absurd. "Bush is more dangerous than Bin Laden." "Iraq is Vietnam all over again." "Guantanamo Bay is just like a concentration camp." These statements usually get you a little free media attention, but they are so patently false as to be bizarre. Eventually, I wrote an article comparing Democrats to Chicken Little.

◆   ◆   ◆

"The Sky Isn't Falling"

Most Americans know the children's stories of Chicken Little and The Boy Who Cried Wolf. Chicken Little, after getting hit on the head by an apple, runs around in a panic insisting that the sky is falling. The Boy Who Cried Wolf constantly raises a false alarm so he can get some attention. If we could get both of these characters in the same room, you would have a meeting of the Democratic Party.

It's expected that political parties will criticize each other. But for criticisms to have any weight, they must be within a stone's throw of credible. In the past month Democrats have accused President Bush of allowing 9/11 to happen, secretly plotting with the Saudis to fix gas prices, stealing $700 million from the Afghanistan war effort, and plotting the Iraq war behind Colin Powell's back. After all the broadsides, an exasperated Powell, exclaimed, "This is getting unreal." Additionally, for the past year, Democrats have been acting like the Patriot Act is the second coming of the Gestapo. For those of us who have read the bill, we know that the Act, which includes numerous judicial oversight and sunshine provisions, does little more than update laws written before the advent of e-mail and cell phones.

When Democrats aren't crying wolf, they're taking a page out of Chicken Little's book. Through exaggerated rhetoric, Democrats respond to every setback by running in circles, waving their hands in the air, screaming "the sky is falling." We have Ted Kennedy insisting Iraq is Vietnam, Joe Biden panicking on CNN, and John Kerry claiming we're headed for economic ruin. Kennedy's comments are simply ignorant. Massive GDP growth, job creation, and every other economic indicator belie Kerry's comments. But putting aside their colossal collective ignorance for a moment, the reality is, America is being challenged with incredibly difficult tasks. There are going to be good days, and bad days. We are going to enjoy successes, and suffer setbacks. Mature adults respond to the successes with satisfaction and the setbacks with renewed determination. What we don't need is melodramatic histrionics from our stunningly adolescent "loyal opposition." For example, no one needed to panic over the exploits of Iraqi cleric Moqtada al-Sadr. We didn't need to elevate this gang thug into a revolutionary. A little bit of patience was all it took to dispatch him with relative ease.

Whether one agrees or disagrees with America's current course of action, at home or abroad, I think everyone agrees we face serious issues. And we need serious leaders to confront these issues. Instead, we have one party making difficult choices in difficult times, and another party so caught up in a rabid hatred of all things Bush, they are threatening the legitimacy of occasionally credible criticisms. America needs a two party system that competes over ideas. However, Democrats have nothing to offer but the mantra "we hate Bush!" That hatred was on full display when the *Daily Collegian*, a Boston student newspaper, ran an editorial claiming that Pat Tillman was an "idiot ... who got what was coming to him [because] he was acting out his macho, patriotic crap." If Democrats (you know, the party of tolerance) want anyone but the foam-at-the-mouth "Deaniacs" to tune them back in, they need to take a deep breath, tone it down, and try to find some marginal foothold on reality. Sen. Joe Lieberman and Tom Daschle took the first steps last week by suggesting that their party ease up on their Iraq and election rhetoric. Thank you Joe and Tom. Opposition parties need to offer alternatives and vision, not vitriolic hatred and irrational hysterics. If you don't believe me, check out Pat Buchannan's address to the Republican National Convention in 1992. It didn't work for Republicans then, and it won't work for Democrats now. Eventually, Americans will come to realize that there is no wolf eating our sheep, and the sky is not falling on our heads.

◆   ◆   ◆

In the end, all of the hypocrisy, hyperbole, and histrionics came to head at the 2004 Democratic National Convention. Democrats had the very difficult job of arguing they could be just as tough as Republicans fighting the war on terror, but at the same time, assail President Bush for his tough stances. And to keep all their special interests groups in line, they had to wrap it all in their traditional populist economic message. A tough job for any party with any candidate. In 2004, just three years following September 11th, it was impossible. After they tried, I wrote about it.

◆   ◆   ◆

"Reflections on the Democratic National Convention"

Now that the Democratic National Convention is past us, it seems that a brief review, or at least a reality check, is in order. The convention got off to a rocky start when anti-war protesters scuffled with an anti-abortion protester and began chanting "silence the fascist." I always find it funny when anti-war protesters use violence to get their message across. Do you think they are even aware of the irony? And since we are discussing irony, let's look at how often liberals use the term "fascist" these days. The term once denoted people who followed the economic/political philosophies of Mussolini and Hitler. Now liberals use it to describe anyone who holds values different from their own. Completely lost upon these people is the irony that using the term "fascist" to stifle the opinions of anyone who disagrees with you is more fascist than any policy one might be protest-ing.

Once the convention did get started, we were greeted with a series of speakers.

The first day included Presidents Carter and Clinton along with Mr. Gore and Mrs. Clinton. In what can only be described as the humor segment of the evening, Mr. Carter opted to lecture on foreign policy. Sometimes jokes don't even need a punch line. Getting a lecture on foreign policy from Mr. Carter is like getting stock advice from Martha Stewart. Of course the foreign policy lan-guage came after he criticized Washington as captured by "lobbyists for the uber-rich." I suppose he was talking about the millions of dollars trial attorneys have funneled to John Edwards.

In a surprising turn, Hollywood actress Glen Close introduced a memorial to 9-11. It was tasteful and moving. But I was left thinking: if the Republicans even mention 9-11 they will be crucified as "capitalizing on the tragedy" or "politiciz-ing the deaths of 1000s of Americans"? The Democratic propaganda machine we call the national media gave the Democrats a free pass. Don't expect the same for the Republicans in September.

The second night of festivities included a speech by Ron Reagan, son of the late president. In listening to his speech I could only feel sadness for his father. I can't imagine that there is anything more painful to a great man than to have a medio-cre son. Everything President Reagan was, his son is not.

The night also included newcomer Barack Obama. He was excellent and so was his speech. The only problem for Democrats was that the first half of his speech (hard work, individual responsibility, limited government) could have been given at the Republican convention.

On the third night, John Edwards had his coming-out ball. Is it just me, or is this guy the Dan Quayle of the Democratic Party? Is there anyone that thinks he is ready to assume the presidency? Command armies? Direct national security? He's barely ready to eat at the adult table during Thanksgiving dinner. Simply put, he's a 22-caliber man in a .357 world.

The convention concluded with John Kerry's acceptance speech. He spent most of his time convincing us that he will be strong on defense and security. A man who spends that much time trying to convince you he has a backbone usually doesn't. President Bush doesn't need to convince us. We already know. Next, Mr. Kerry told us he would rebuild alliances around the world; followed by a scathing attack on Saudi Arabia. Memo to Mr. Kerry: it will probably be easier to rebuild alliances if you don't insult, in front of 200 million Americans, our most powerful ally in the region. I guess when you tell the French to go to hell, its unilateralism. When you do it to the Saudis, its diplomacy.

But through it all was one simple message: John Kerry is a veteran and that makes him the most qualified to be president. This new-found Democratic concern for veterans is shallow and opportunistic. If Democrats gave a hoot about veterans, we would all be saying "President Dole."

◆   ◆   ◆

A good place to finish up this chapter is with a piece I wrote titled "The No-Choice Pro-Choice Party." When you spend as much time on a college campus as I do, you can't avoid the politics of abortion. There are lots of sexually active young adults dominating the landscape and many professional women who chose a time-consuming career. Even the conservative leaning professors, as few as there are, tend to be "socially liberal, economically conservative." So, you hear the words "pro-choice" a lot when you get into political debates at a university. "I'm a Democrat because I believe people have the right to choose" was levied at me in the hallway one day … the same day President Bush was pushing his new social security plan to give people a choice on how they want to invest their retirement money. I was struck by how anti-choice the Democratic Party really is. Thus, another column was born.

◆   ◆   ◆

"The No-Choice Pro-Choice Party"

I am always amazed when someone refers to the Democratic Party as the "party of choice." It's like referring to Seattle as a "bastion of conservatives." The Democrats claim on that label of "choice" comes from their abortion stance. But, beyond that one issue, the Democratic Party is generally hostile to individual choice. Other than abortion, Democrats rarely get beyond their paternalistic, government knows best, you're too ignorant to make any life decisions, ideology. Let's look at a few election year issues.

Vouchers and charter schools are a good place to start. Here is a simple idea. Let parents have a *choice* where to send their kids to school. It is a financially neutral policy that puts a little market pressure on teachers and schools to perform better. Yet, ask Democrats about vouchers and you would think someone suggested abolishing the public school system. You see, for Democrats, school choice is just fine for rich, white folks who live in urban environments. They can send their kids to expensive private schools. But give that same choice to poor black parents, and hey, you're just talking crazy now. Despite the fact that polling suggests Black Americans support vouchers, the white, Democratic, liberal elite can't shed its plantation mentality. You poor people just sit back and let the National Education Association make all your education decisions for you.

Or, how about social security? President Bush has long sought the right for people to invest a paltry 5% of their social security withholding into private stock accounts. Citizens would actually have a *choice* about their retirement accounts. [Before you claim right-wing extremism: socialist Sweden allows private investment accounts.] But again, ask John Kerry about social security choice and you would think we were raiding grandma's pension plan. Despite the fact that the Baby Boom generation is getting older and we are faced with the certainty of higher taxes or smaller benefits, Democrats prefer to stick their heads in the sand and pretend there is no problem. But they're probably right. How would dumb people like us know how to invest our own money? Thank goodness my government is there to make all the complicated decisions for me.

Most recently President Bush gave senior citizens a *choice* regarding Medicare plans. They can stay with the same plan they have had since the Johnson Administration, or they can move to other private plans. Again, ask Democrats about Medicare reform and you would think we booted grandma to the curb and stole her prescription drugs. But of course, my grandparents, who survived the Depression and WWII, can't make decisions about their own health care. They need Ted Kennedy for that.

I sincerely don't understand the hypocrisy of the Democratic Party when it comes to the issue of choice. How can anyone believe that human beings are capable of making profound decisions about continuing or terminating a pregnancy, but don't believe that same person can make decisions about schools, health care, and retirement plans? Is it that terminating a pregnancy is a trivial choice compared to choosing a health care plan? Either you have faith in human beings to make life-effecting decisions or you don't. But how can you look someone in the eye and say "I trust you to decide the fate of your fetus, but not the fate of your retirement plan."

The irony of this hypocrisy is compounded by the fact that Democrats are currently campaigning to "take their country back." The scary part is that they mean it. Their utopia is a government where, from cradle to grave, the Democratic Party makes all your choices for you. Maybe that's what they mean by being "the party of choice." Oh boy, my life run like the DMV.

Come November, I'm going to exercise my choice to vote Republican. If I don't, it may be the last choice I get to make.

◆   ◆   ◆

In the end, everything turned out okay. The American people kept their heads on their shoulders and didn't buy the hype. President Bush was the first president since his father in 1988 elected (in this case re-elected) with over a majority of the vote. His 3,000,000 vote margin of victory was not a Reaganesque mandate, but it was a notice to the Left that Americans did not want the Patriot Act scrapped, all the terrorists released from Guantanamo Bay, nor a revival of Lyndon Johnson's social welfare state.

But victory at the polls doesn't mean smooth sailing for the next four years. You still have to deal with politics, the media, interparty fights, and the French. Good thing there are more chapters to this book.

5

Republicans

A Republican friend of mine once jokingly commented, "The Republican Party is a 'big tent' party, it's just the door in that is so small." Behind the humor is a little truth. One of the larger dilemmas that the Republican Party faces is the tension between the libertarian-market-friendly conservatives and the family-values-social-conservatives. Some people are Republicans because they want low taxes, limited government, and would like to see bureaucracies like the Department of Labor and Industries fall into the Puget Sound. If it won't fall into the Sound, they would be happy to push it in. Other people are Republicans because they oppose abortion, gay marriage, and stem cell research. Two agendas … one party. Never an easy task.

From a public relations perspective, however, the larger problem that confronts the Republican Party is overcoming the media and academic stereotypes with which they are labeled. There are so many stereotypes that float around about my party. We are prudish. We are stingy. We have first names like Thurston and often have roman numerals after our last name. Each morning we read the Wall Street Journal and drink prune juice. Just for the record, I have never had a glass of prune juice.

Or, Republicans are accused of clinging to the past. We haven't earned the right to be called "progressive" because we hate change. Watch just about any movie and it becomes clear that most of Hollywood thinks that Republicans sit on the porch every evening sipping a glass of port and pining for the days of *Leave it to Beaver*. Golly Wally, that's a load of hewey.

Like all stereotypes, if you dig deep enough you can find an individual or small group of people who exhibit the characteristics of the stereotype. Those groups tend to be magnified and manipulated in the media to maintain the impression CNN wants you to have of Republicans. In university settings, Republicans or conservatives suffer stereotypes as well. We are the "party of the rich," the "party of white males," the "party of bible thumpers," or the "party of corporate power." In Eugene, where I went to graduate school, if a student blames any political crisis on corporations or the "religious right" they will pass the test. They don't need any data or facts, just an *X-Files* type conspiracy about corporate power wedded to the religious right gets them to the A+ they want.

In one of my first columns about the Republican Party, I challenged the notion that Democrats are a progressive party and that Republicans cling to the status quo. In "Conservative as Liberal" I argued that since 1970, it has been the Republican Party that has been the party of new ideas. In contrast, it has been Democrats who have clung to the ideas of the New Deal and refused to look at new solutions for a changing environment.

◆   ◆   ◆

"Conservative as Liberal"

Politics, reduced to its basic core, is a battle over resources and ideas. While the former is eternal and needs no catalyst, the latter is most productive if, at least, two sides are engaged in the process. In the past 40 years, the Democrat Party has been highly active in the battle for resources (usually taking the resources of others) but they have been nearly absent in the battle of ideas.

It wasn't always this way. When FDR came to the White House in 1932, he brought with him the intellectual elite of the nation. Academics from all over the country abandoned their jobs to come to Washington and offer new ideas for governance. FDR made the Democratic Party the "party of ideas." And for 40 years, Democrats earned that title. That is not to say that all their ideas were good. Many were terrible. But at least they were trying. At least they were willing to join the dance.

Unfortunately, those days are long gone. The last new idea from Democrats came out of the Johnson Administration. This point was made painfully obvious to me when Democrats suggested an increase in the minimum wage as a way to improve the economy. Here is an idea 80 years old and so counter-productive and incalculably stupid that only the 12 members of the O.J. jury think it's a good idea. But lacking any new ideas, they continue to offer a 1930s solution for a 21st century economy.

In contrast, the last four decades have illustrated the Republican Party's virtual monopoly on reform movements. It was Republican state governors who pushed the welfare reform movement of the 1980s. Conservative think tanks provided the intellectual arguments for the tort reform movement that began in the 1990s. Today, it's Republicans tackling education reform with new ideas such as charter schools, magnet schools, and vouchers. Yesterday, it was Ronald Reagan who spent the political capital to reform our marginal tax system that was destroying incentive. And presently, we see President Bush rising to the challenge of Medicare and Social Security reform. Once thought untouchable and unfixable, Bush used his first term to modernize Medicare and he is using his second to try and revolutionize Social Security.

But to be fair, just like the Democrats of the 1930s, not every reform idea floated by Republicans has been a good idea. But at least Republicans are "in the arena" making proposals, challenging the status quo. What new ideas have Democrats offered in the last 40 years? To every crisis their response is the same: either spend more money or scare people away from change. We tried spending more money on education for 40 years to no effect. Maybe it's time for a new idea. And now we face a failing Social Security system. Scaring senior citizens has not made the problem go away. Yet, what is the Democratic response to partial privatization? Do nothing. Bury your head in the sand. Raise payroll taxes. Scare voters into believing Grandma will be out on the streets.

To see how far they have fallen, Democrats need look no farther than inside themselves. When the intellectual foundation of your party is articulated by Michael Moore and Al Franken, you know you have fallen into the abyss. How is it that an ex-writer for Saturday Night Live and a Hollywood malcontent have come to symbolize the extent of your party's cerebral capabilities? What has led a once vibrant party to become so intellectually bankrupt that their creativity is limited to writing bigger checks and fear mongering?

Where "liberal" once meant progressive and "conservative" once meant to embrace the status quo, the last 40 years have shown just the opposite. President Bush summarized this point concisely when he noted, "A litany of complaints is not a plan." His comments are just as true for domestic policy as they were for

Iraq. As we head into the New Year, maybe Democrats should celebrate by coming up with some new ideas.

◆   ◆   ◆

Another stereotype the media tries to pin on Republicans is that we are all knuckle-dragging Neanderthals who treat the Bible as the only source of information, hate science, and would like to see the Constitution replaced by the Old Testament. Contrary to what you may read in the New York Times, there are lots of religious people who work in the scientific fields and more importantly, Republicans value the separation of church and state just as much as liberals. Yes, many Republicans feel it's not a crime to pray at school functions or for firefighters to put up a Christmas tree in their station, and most Republicans don't think the Pledge of Allegiance is unconstitutional because it includes the phrase "under God" in it. That doesn't mean, however, that we want a Taliban-like religious Gestapo set up in America.

Democrats, on the other hand, tend to panic at the first sight of any overt religious behavior. If 3rd graders sing *God Rest Ye Merry Gentlemen* at a school Christmas program ... oops, I mean "Holiday program" they feel the immediate need to take large amounts of Prozac. Pick up any junior high history book when you get a chance. They have replaced "Before Christ" (B.C.) with "Before Common Era" (B.C.E.). By SHEER coincidence, B.C.E starts the same year some Jewish kid was born to parents named Mary and Joseph in Bethlehem about 20 centuries ago. What's important here is that teachers don't ever have to say "Christ" in class anymore.

It was with this Democratic hyper-sensitivity towards any type of religious speech or behavior in mind that I wrote "The Puritans are Coming." The title invoked the image of a Paul Revere type racing through downtown Seattle screaming, "Religious people are coming ... Religious people are coming!" Oh the horror! The more immediate reason for the column was to respond to the panic that was consuming media types when they got exit polling data from the 2004 Bush victory that indicated 22% of people chose "moral values" as the most important criteria when making their presidential vote. As they usually do, the media misinterpreted the data to conclude that armies of religious zealots were marching on Washington and that we were all a fifty-cent cab ride from the return of The Scarlet Letter.

◆   ◆   ◆

"The Puritans are Coming"

There is a panic in the "blue" cities of America. Why the fear? All the post-election analysis has led reporters and political pundits to believe that an impending theocracy is just around the corner. Listening to Wolf Blitzer you would assume those Bible thumping zealots he calls Republicans are just itching to re-instigate the Spanish Inquisition.

The more I hang around politically active people, the more I come to realize that political adversaries are all too willing to give in to the most outrageous caricatures of their opponents. To many conservatives I know, all you have to do is scratch a liberal and there is a socialist underneath just yearning to seize everyone's private property and impose a Swedish-like welfare state upon us. Conversely, most liberals I know firmly believe that if you scratch a conservative, underneath is a Confederate flag waving religious zealot who secretly admires the Taliban.

Both characterizations are overblown. Most liberals have a healthy respect for private property, individualism, and even free markets. And most conservatives value the separation of church and state and oppose excessive state-based moralism. The reason these stereotypes have experienced a recent renaissance was the surprising presidential exit poll results showing 22% of all voters identified "moral values" as their most important issue. Upon hearing such numbers, liberals felt their worst fears had come to pass. Surely it was only a matter of time before the religious right started calling in favors and demanding the Constitution be replaced with the Old Testament.

The problem is that these exit polls are very misleading. As any pollster knows, respondents are highly susceptible to the suggestions of the pollster. Political scientists know from previous research that if a pollster asks a question, and then provides a list of possible answers, people will pick from those answers. If the pollsters had listed "witchcraft" as an answer, about 5% of people would have selected that reason for voting for a candidate. Experienced pollsters know that it is better to ask open-ended questions in which the individual has to come up with his own answer. Gary Langer of ABC polling notes that in all the pre-election open-ended polling, "moral values" never scored above single digits.

The second problem with the media's interpretation of the exit polls is that "moral values" is not a concrete term. When people identify "the economy" as their number one issue, we know what they mean. However, "moral values" means different things to different people. Some respondents may have been referring to gay marriage or abortion. But other respondents could have been referring to access to health care or civil rights. We simply don't know. In case you doubt, about 22% of Washington voters selected "moral values" and that state went for Kerry.

And finally, polling also suffers from what is termed "social desirability bias." This means people pick answers that make them look good to the pollster. If you ask people what is important to them: getting a new car or helping the poor, they will answer, "helping the poor." It makes them look like a good person. When you have an exit poll that lists "the economy" (read: I'm selfish and care about my financial situation) or "moral values" (read: I'm a good person that leads a clean life) it should not be surprising that 22% of the people picked moral values.

These results should not be interpreted to believe that there is a fundamentalist revolution on the horizon. Republicans don't want a theocracy any more than Democrats want communism. Andrew Kohut of PEW Research noted that President Bush won because all types of conservatives increased their turnout, including libertarian and small business owner Republicans, not just evangelicals as the media seems to suggest. In the coming months, the media and Democrats are going to try and scare you into believing Republicans want to bring back a world reminiscent of The Scarlet Letter. Don't believe either of them.

◆   ◆   ◆

Almost all political parties are made up of two factions. On one end of the spectrum, they have their uncompromising members, what I call the "zealots" who would "rather be right than win." At the other end, they have their more moderate membership. These are party members who are "willing to compromise to win." Every political party must walk a fine line to appease both their moderate and extreme wings. Many of you may remember Howard Dean's campaign slogan of "I represent the Democratic wing of the Democratic Party." He was trying to say, "I will represent the liberal wing of the party while all these other guys are just trying to be Republican-lite." In early 2008, Rudy Giuliani was suffering the same problem but in the opposite direction. The moderate Republicans were willing to compromise on social values with Giuliani because they thought he could win, but the hard-core right was unwilling to give on certain social issues, even if it meant they might lose the Presidential election.

When President Bush took office in 2001, he had done a pretty good job of navigating the minefield that can be coalition politics. He kept the hard right in line with his views on abortion, stem cells, and faith-based grant programs. At the same time, he was advocating huge increases in education spending (No Child Left Behind) and promoting a prescription drug program for seniors. These types of programs attract moderates and independents. But winners in politics always struggle with two issues. First, they become enamored with winning over their enemies. They begin to think they can make friends of their enemies. The AARP, NAACP, and the NEA are NEVER going to like Republicans. Period. But Bush tried anyway and it pulled him away from his conservative mission.

The second phenomenon that erodes a wining political party is that they get captured by the very institutions they sought to capture. It is easy to "run against Washington" until you "become Washington." Seduced by the allure of power. Corrupted by the desire to maintain a majority and too timid to confront the divisive issues of our times, a party of principle can become a party of expediency. Long before the disastrous elections of 2006, I saw the erosion of the Republican Party's conservative principles and took them to task for it. In "Is the Republican Revolution Over?" I warned Republicans that if they spent too much time trying to make friends with the Left, they would lose the soul of the party. When millions of Republicans stayed home on election night in November 2006, I think they proved me right. In the end, the party of Lincoln forgot what Lincoln had told them over a century earlier,

"I am not bound to win, but I am bound to be true. I am not bound to succeed, but I am bound to live by the light that I have. I must stand with anybody that stands right, and stand with him while he is right, and part with him when he goes wrong."

◆   ◆   ◆

"Is the Republican Revolution Over?"

For those of you who tune in to my column each month for a little "liberal bashing," turn away now. This is not the column for you. As painful as it might be, it's time to take my own party to task.

Traditionally, the Republican Party has portrayed itself as the party of fiscal discipline. For two decades, Republican members of Congress and presidential candidates condemned "big spending liberals" who "waste your tax dollars." However, this type of rhetoric and voting behavior happened while they were the minority party in Washington. But in 1994, Republicans swept to majority status in both houses of Congress, and since then, overspending hasn't seemed like such a bad idea anymore.

There is a dirty little secret in Washington, D.C. The amount of federal spending has nothing to do with ideology. On what we spend our money, there is some debate. On HOW we pay for that spending there is considerable debate. But in general, high spending favors incumbents regardless of party. The party in power always wants to stay in power. And the surest way to stay in power is to provide all the "pork" you can to as many constituents as you can. Need the elderly vote? How does $600 billion for prescription drugs sound? Come on. If Clinton had proposed that bill, my party would have screamed "socialized medicine!" Need the rural vote? How about $20 billion in farm subsidies (even though most of those subsidies go to large corporations and not small farmers)? And on and on.

A few weeks ago, President Bush released his $2.5 trillion 2006 budget. True to his word, he made some effort to reduce wasteful spending by cutting 150 government programs (which amounted to a whopping .8% of the budget). With expected hypocrisy, Democrats assailed every cut, despite having spent the last four years criticizing the deficit. The Democratic mayor of Baltimore went so far as to compare the cuts to the 9/11 attacks! I have come to expect this type of ridiculous hyperbole from liberals. What I found so disturbing was that joining the chorus (with more appropriate rhetoric) were many Republican members of Congress who had one of their local projects cut. Republicans from the Pacific Northwest didn't want any increases in their subsidized water bills. Midwest Republicans didn't want any decreases in their farm subsidies. Are these Congressmen doing their jobs? Sure. They are elected to protect our interests. But, their actions show me that when voters say they want less spending, they really mean they want less spending on other people, not less spending for themselves. It is always easy to be for a balanced budget and a smaller federal government in the abstract. But when it comes down to actually shrinking the size of the federal government, everyone wants to balance the budget on the backs of other people.

It's not difficult for parties in the minority to decry federal spending. Less spending means angry people and angry people turn minority parties into majority parties. It is more difficult for majority parties to hold the line on spending. They are faced with paradoxical political demands. On one hand, people hate having their taxes raised. But they also hate having their benefits and government programs reduced. So in the end, it's always easier to give voters everything they want, leave their taxes alone, and just borrow the difference. But then citizens complain about deficits! Voters are often quick to criticize the hypocrisy of elected officials. But what they often forget is that elected officials are simply trying to meet the hypocritical demands of their voters.

In the next few months, the Republican Party is going to have to make some tough decisions. Is fiscal discipline going to be empty rhetoric, or are they going to put my money where their mouth is? The Gingrich revolution promised us a smaller and less expensive government. They told us that if Republicans ever controlled the White House and both chambers of Congress at the same time, we would see results. Well, all those things have come true and I'm waiting for the results. The government is growing faster under President Bush than it did under President Clinton.

If we are going to cut the deficit, we are all going to have to accept fewer benefits (even political science professors at state funded universities). That means our members of Congress must say, "I'll accept cuts to my district if you'll accept cuts to yours." But more importantly, it's going to require voters to say, "I understand that you had to cut some of my programs, and I won't hold it against you in the next election." If we expect integrity from our elected officials, we have to exhibit it ourselves.

◆   ◆   ◆

Just before the 2006, elections, a lot of my liberal friends were calling President Bush "the worst president ever." Let's see, I said. No terrorist attack on American soil since 9/11, one of the fastest growing economies the nation had ever seen, billions of dollars to stop AIDS in Africa, education reform, and tax cuts for working families. Yep, that sounds just terrible. So just before the 2006 elections I tried to take a fair look at what Bush had accomplished and where he had failed.

◆   ◆   ◆

"Bush in His Sixth Year"

Former Speaker of the House Tip O'Neil is famous for asserting that "all politics is local." However, as mid-term elections approach, it seems this year's electoral contests will be more of a referendum on the Bush Administration than a reflection of local politics. So, it only seems fair to take up that challenge and offer a reflection on the successes and failures of President Bush as he enters his sixth year in office.

President Bush can legitimately claim some successes. His greatest success is that not a single terrorist attack has taken place on American soil since September 11th. In the days that followed those horrific events, people assumed it was a question of "when" not "if." Bush has proven them wrong. Not a single American has died on our soil at the hands of Osama bin Laden or any other fanatic. Bush promised to protect the American people and he has kept that promise. Only the bitterest partisan would deny the President's right to claim this victory.

He can claim the economy as a success as well. Having weathered a storm of financial shocks caused by September 11th, a series of accounting scandals that took place before his watch, and a cyclical downturn in the economy, we are experiencing an exceptionally robust economy. Unemployment is about as low as it can go. Inflation has stayed down despite significant GDP growth rates, and interest rates are holding. Democrats didn't want to lower taxes, but Bush browbeat them into it and we are all better off for it. Despite the tax cuts, tax revenue is up and the deficit is shrinking. Only the most ignorant partisan would deny the economy is a success.

His Supreme Court appointees belong in the success column too. He found two nominees who had actually read the Constitution and agreed not to legislate from the bench. It's been a century since we have had a president accomplish that.

President Bush must also take the blame for serious failures as well. He has completely dropped the ball on illegal immigration. As millions of illegal immigrants stream across the border overwhelming our schools, hospitals, and social welfare programs, Bush has not used his political clout to push Congress to meet the problem. A few months ago, thousands of non-citizens waived Mexican flags in the streets chanting "today we march, tomorrow we vote" and everyone heard the chilling threat in that statement except residents of the White House. When I drive to Yakima now, most of the radio stations are Hispanic, the signs in box stores are in Spanish and fast food restaurants try to take my order in Spanish until I correct them. But President Bush doesn't want to lose the vote gains he has made in the Hispanic community and it's only a matter of time before we learn about the long-term price of political pandering.

Bush must also take responsibility for the massive increase in the social welfare state. Not since another Texan occupied the White House have we seen such a significant increase in the size of government. Lyndon Johnson brought us the "Great Society" and George Bush brought us a $600 billion unfunded liability in his prescription drug plan. Ronald Reagan is rolling over in his grave and Franklin Roosevelt is laughing in his. It is hard to look people in the eye and insist that the Republican Party is the party of limited government after the past few years.

Then there are some policies where it is simply too soon to tell. The No Child Left Behind Act belongs here. Bush had the courage to demand results from our public education system. But we will have to wait for comprehensive studies to see if it had any impact.

I put Iraq in this category as well. Bush was too quick to declare victory and the Democrats were too quick to declare defeat. But history has a way of walking to the beat of its own drum. It will probably fall to the next generation to decide if Iraq was a success or a failure. Until then, we can debate it till we are blue (or red) in the face. Or we can just vote on November 7th.

◆　　　◆　　　◆

Where else can I finish a chapter on Republicans than with Ronald Reagan? He is, and will continue to be, the face of the Republican Party in the 21th Century. If there was a Republican Mount Rushmore, there would be only three faces: Abraham Lincoln, Teddy Roosevelt, and Ronald Reagan. Reagan died while I was a professor at Central Washington University and I can tell you that academics harbor an intense dislike for our 40th President. He was a cowboy. He was stupid. He was a war monger. He didn't care about poor people. The list goes on and on. But that's not what angers them so much. What really kills them is that he was right. Reagan sought peace through strength and got it. Reagan sought prosperity through tax cuts and deregulation and found it. Reagan spoke about the never-ending spirit of America and helped create it. I can tell you that nothing angers a critic more than the success of their adversaries. Reagan was right, and the left will never forgive him for it—especially the left that lives in Sociology departments around the county. When Reagan died, I saved my column to remind my fellow citizens what he did and meant for this country.

◆   ◆   ◆

"Reagan's Legacy"

The world lost a giant this week, and America lost a friend. Our 40th President, Ronald Reagan, lost his long battle with Alzheimer's disease. In the centuries to come, the world will only remember three presidents from the 20th Century: Woodrow Wilson, Franklin Roosevelt, and Ronald Reagan. Let me tell you why they will remember Reagan.

Most of the great leaders that find their way to history's pedestal saved the world from external enemies: barbarians at the gate, dictators, or religious zealots. Reagan, in contrast, saved the world from bad ideas. Coming out of WWII, the world's great democracies elected to put their faith in the state, in collectivism, and the idea that centralized bureaucracies could provide humanity with never ending prosperity. But of course, the academics, the Marxists, and utopians had once again missed the mark. The commanding heights of society must be held by individuals, not governments.

Reagan knew this, and with a sole ally in Margaret Thatcher, had the courage to tell the world it was wrong. That true human freedom could only be achieved by unleashing the enormous potential of individuals, unchained from government restraints. At the time, his words were sacrilege. But like all great visionaries, Reagan understood that good ideas, regardless of their unpopularity, will eventually win out over bad ideas. He showed us some universal truths: F.A. Hayek and Milton Friedman were right and John Keynes and Gunnar Myrdal were wrong; incentives are more moving than coercion; individuals are more enlightened than committees; markets are more efficient than governments, and governments don't create wealth, people do.

His lessons were so powerful that he did what few men ever do. He changed the minds of his opponents. Today, capitalism and democracy permeate Eastern Europe. Modern Chinese leaders sound more like Jefferson than Mao. Democrats now embrace free trade, deregulation, a limited social welfare state, and oppose deficits. How the world has changed since 1980.

I don't subscribe to the view that Regan "won" the Cold War. It was a team effort. He was a significant member of that team, but the team also included an energetic Pope John Paul II, a rebellious Lech Walesa, a realistic Michael Gorbachev, and 50 years of bipartisan foreign policy.

Reagan's greatest contribution, however, was the revival of the American spirit. Following the 1970s Americans had lost hope and confidence. Reagan, through sheer force of will, brought America back to its feet. When everyone else had doubts, he still believed in the shining "city on the hill." He showed us that the real test of leadership was the ability to infuse the people with optimism, energy, and spirit. I work in a field where most people are pretty jaded. Seeped in cynicism, academics tend to reject the notion that presidents can inspire their countrymen. Talking about hope and optimism appears unsophisticated. It lacks the nuance of an intellectual. Most of my colleagues have a dim view of Reagan: honest but simple. But sometimes, the simplest truths carry the greatest power. Reagan knew right from wrong, freedom from tyranny, and hope from despondency. These simple truths led a man to lead a country to lead a world. And we are all better off because he did.

There is an endless story. It is the story of human freedom, hope, and opportunity. Few men that have walked the stage of history have had the courage or vision to contribute a chapter. But of our recently lost President we can say this; his chapter will be forever etched in souls of men and women who know the value of liberty. And I will read it to my students, my children, and my grandchildren.

6

Europe

Maybe the title of this chapter is a little unfair. I mean, should countries like Poland, Ireland, the Czech Republic, and England be lumped into the same category as France? Probably not, but I couldn't think of a better title and it's my book.

Title aside, there is just something about the European way of looking at the world that gets under my skin. Part of it is the way they drip in self-righteousness. Part of it is the glee with which they criticize Americans for tackling difficult responsibilities that they themselves have ducked. Maybe it's the condescension with which they look down their noses at us unsophisticated cowboys.

I am fond of the statement, "only the impotent and naïve have the luxury of self-righteousness." I think it's a good description of Europe. They love to complain about injustices in the world, but they seldom want to do anything about them. Talking about injustice makes them look morally superior. Doing something requires them to get their hands dirty. In concrete terms, Europeans love United Nations resolutions, but hate following up on them. In some ways, Europeans act like frustrated adolescents who complain about injustice in the world. They can pound the table, but they don't really have the power or the will to do anything about it.

In the first of many columns about Europe, I tackled the issue of European "sophistication" versus American "crassness." I saw it a little differently, and said so.

◆　　◆　　◆

"European Sophistication?"

For the past few weeks my wife and I have been tromping through the forests of Banff in Alberta, Canada. After a couple nights sleeping on the ground waiting for a grizzly bear to come eat us, we decided to spend a few nights in a Calgary hotel. The sojourn to a foreign land (if Canada qualifies) has been enlightening. You get to watch the evening news from a completely different perspective. In our hotel we got to catch up on the Olympics and watch newscasts from the BBC as well as Canadian stations.

I flipped on the news and watched a story about the Iraqi soccer team. The anchor was enthusiastically describing how the players no longer feared the sadistic torture of Uday Hussein if they lost a match. Part of the program showed the various torture devices Hussein used on his players. There was no mention of the United States and President Bush, or how his decisions were the reason Iraqis were no longer being tortured. Immediately following this story was an update on the American "occupation of Iraq" that was continuing to "inflict destruction on the lives of Iraqi citizens." It was almost as if they could not grasp the connection between the two stories. In the end, the need to hold on to their self-righteousness was more important than accepting the possibility that America might not be the great Satan of the world.

I also got to watch numerous updates about how American athletes were continually booed by the fans in Athens. Paul Hamm was booed. Rulon Gardner was booed. The American volleyball team was booed. These stories got me to thinking about one of the great myths about European and American cultures. We are constantly told by liberals and media elites that Europeans, Asians, and Latin Americans are more sophisticated than Americans. We simple-minded Americans can only see black and white while foreigners can see shades of grey. In essence, Americans are too simplistic for the art of diplomacy.

But then I thought back to the Olympic Games in Salt Lake City and the controversy over the pair's figure skating. After it was discovered that a French judge cheated, a second gold medal was awarded to the Canadian team. However, throughout all the controversy, the American audience was sophisticated enough not to take out their anger on the Russian skaters. We knew that no matter how much we disagreed with the decision, it was surely not the fault of these hardworking athletes. They were cheered and treated with respect. Now jump forward four years to Athens, Greece and we see European fans booing the American Paul Hamm because they don't like the judging; as if Hamm or even an American judge was responsible for the mistake. Who is being simplistic here?

This incident got me thinking about how the American soccer team was treated in Mexico City a few months ago. During a match between Mexico and the United States, 100,000 Mexican fans started chanting "Osama, Osama." How sophisticated that they would chant the name of a psychotic who just murdered 3,000 people. Can you imagine someone chanting "Adolf" at an Israeli sporting event? Compare this behavior to the way American fans have embraced the Iraqi soccer team. Even though Iraqi citizens are still killing our soldiers, we cheered the success of their team. That's seeing shades of grey.

The last story I saw before heading back into the wilds and bears, was about a Greek protest against Colin Powell that delayed a few Olympic events. I wish I could have asked the protesters a few questions. Did you ever protest against Saddam Hussein when he invaded Iran? Did you take to the streets when he invaded Kuwait? Did you march when he gassed the Kurds? Why is it that a murderous dictator never raises the hackles of these sophisticated Europeans, but American armies who never take anything but a few acres to bury their dead, rile them to their core? Maybe the most simplistic behavior in the world today is the irrational and petulant anti-Americanism that pervades the rest of the world.

◆   ◆   ◆

If there is one lesson the world was supposed to learn from the events that led up to World War II, it was that appeasement doesn't work. Since it is European appeasement that usually leads to American deaths, Americans have learned the lesson of 1939. We see a bully in the world, we step in. Better to confront a small-time bully now than a well-armed bully later. This philosophy doesn't always make us the most popular country in the world, but it does make the world a safer place.

I am not entirely convinced that Europeans have learned this lesson. Each time we see a new aggressor on the stage, we see Europeans who want to make nice with the enemy. This bury your head in the sand approach rarely, if ever works, but they keep hoping. As we look out at the world today, a world in which North Korea and Iran are actively seeking nuclear weapons, who in Europe is willing to stand up and say "no"? The silence is deafening. Iran knows that Europe will wring its hands, protest diplomatically at the U.N. and in the end, do absolutely nothing about the problem. Iran can just wait them out. Once they have nuclear weapons in hand, it won't really matter anyway.

But if ever there was evidence that the lessons of World War II were lost upon some Europeans, we need look no further than the way the Spanish reacted to the Madrid rail bombings on 3/11 of 2004. At the time, Prime Minister José Aznar led the Spanish government and he had been an enthusiastic partner with Bush and Blair in Iraq. Now it was election time and the Spanish people were going to have their say. Should Spain stay and help, or abandon their friends in need. The polls suggested the Spanish would show a little backbone and stay. Then Al Qaeda stepped in. They bombed several rail cars in downtown Madrid, killing hundreds of people. How did the people of Spain react? Did they show fortitude and make it clear they would not be pushed around by terrorists? No. They folded like a cheap suit. They ran like lemmings. They embarrassed themselves by turning the government over to a socialist who promptly removed all Spanish troops from Iraq. Neville Chamberlain would have been so proud.

◆   ◆   ◆

"Spanish Surrender"

Last week, international terrorist organization Al Qaeda scored its biggest success since September 11th. Their success wasn't the cowardly bombings that took place in the railways of Spain. Their victory was handed to them by the Spanish people. In response to the bombings that killed 200 people, the Spanish electorate announced their surrender by voting out the ruling party. Not since the Europeans abandoned the Czechoslovakian people to the invading hordes of Nazis in 1939, has a greater act of collective cowardice been committed. Osama Bin Laden must be dancing in his cave realizing how easy it is to topple a European government.

When President Bush initiated the war in Iraq, I was not surprised that there was little support in Europe. Yes, the Brits stood by us. But they're a people with a history of courage. They, unlike most of their European brethren, have something we Americans like to call "backbone." But I must confess I was surprised at the support from the Spanish government. Polls showed that 90 percent of Spaniards opposed America's actions in Iraq. But Prime Minister José Aznar decided to do what was right instead of what was popular. Other than Presidents Harry Truman and our own current president, that is a rare quality in the politics of any nation. But stand by us they did.

But last week, the Spanish people got hit by Al Qaeda. And their response was one of the most shameful I have ever seen. Can you imagine in the days following September 11th, 2001 if President Bush had announced that we were giving into Al Qaeda demands? Can you see our President speaking from the Oval Office surrendering to bin Laden? Can you imagine the American people, even the most liberal peace activists among us, voting to abandon our support for Israel in hopes it would prevent future attacks? As a coach I have seen players quit on the field. As a teacher I have seen students give up. As a historian, I know that generals have surrendered. But I have never seen an entire nation raise a white flag so quickly, and so willingly.

There are some among us that wonder why America is such a lone wolf in the world. They ask why we are not more like our European allies. The answer is brutal but clear: America does not seek the leadership of Europe because they have no leadership to offer. Caught up in their bourgeois pettiness; more concerned with criticizing others than manning a post; they are content to sleep under the blanket of security and freedom that America provides while at the same time criticizing the manner in which we provide it.

In watching with horror the Spanish response to Al Qaeda, I begin to ponder with fear what my nation's response will be to our next terrorist attack. Will we follow our history of stubborn resilience? Will we rise to the challenge as we always have? Or is that the old America? Are we still the America "that shall pay any price, bear any burden, meet any hardship, support any friend, oppose any foe, in order to assure the survival and the success of liberty?" Or, have we modified our motto? Do we only defend liberty when it does not interfere with our 401ks, job markets, stock markets, and our disposable income? I know that my nation is far from perfect. But I hope that I will never have to live through a self-inflicted national humiliation like the one the Spanish people imposed on themselves last week. In times of crisis, I hope that Americans will always find the "backbone" that so many of our European allies have stowed away in museums and history books.

◆   ◆   ◆

Sometimes I just flat out step in it. By "it" I mean a big steaming pile of "it." In October, 2005 two young Muslim kids in the suburbs of Paris, France were running from the police. They tried to hide in an electrical box. They both got electrocuted and died. A tragic story. What followed was, in many ways, a worse story.

The Muslim immigrant community was outraged. They started burning buildings and cars. Worse for the French government, the violence was spreading, eventually reaching 15 communities. What were these young immigrants so angry about? They couldn't find jobs. They had to live in ghettos. They didn't like the way they were being treated in France. When I heard this I had two thoughts—Of course you can't find jobs, it's France and they have the dumbest economic policies on the planet, and second, if you don't like it, you are always welcome to go home. Don't let the door hit you in the butt on the way out.

I am always shocked and offended when immigrants complain about the country they immigrated to, particularly if they immigrated there illegally. Talk about hutzpah! Here you had a group of people who *willing* left their home country because things were so bad. They arrived in France, started partaking of the social welfare system, and then complained about it. It started reminding me a lot of what I was seeing on my own Southern boarder. It was one thing for illegal immigrants to assert themselves, it was something completely different when they started marching in the street, demanding their "rights" and pulling down the American flag and replacing it with the Mexican flag. Watching my TV and seeing Muslim immigrants burn down the cities of their host country made me wonder how long it would be before I saw something similar in my own backyard.

So, I stepped in it. I wrote about the need for cultural assimilation of immigrants … and I did it in a college town where "multiculturalism" and "diversity" are a religion. Once again I was earning my heretic credentials and this time, I was going to get punched in the teeth for it. Let's start with what I actually wrote.

◆　　◆　　◆

"Paris is Burning"

We have always known that some things don't go together well: cats and dogs, oil and water, the Democratic Party and common sense. But, after watching the events in France over the past few weeks, we can confidently add another to the list: multiculturalism and open borders. As residents in Paris watch their city go up in flames, they are being forced to reconsider their immigration and assimilation policies.

Cultural assimilation is the process by which societies teach new members (children and immigrants) the rules, norms, and values of the existing society. For children, we use schools, media, and churches to teach them our history, symbolism, and acceptable behavior. For immigrants, we use a more formal procedure. For example, in the United States, you must pass a test before you can become a citizen. Societies that engage in assimilation procedures are stable and secure. Societies that don't are called Yugoslavia. If you don't believe me, go find Yugoslavia on a map. I'll wait.

Unfortunately, Americans need to take note of what is happening in Paris. As a nation, we used to do an excellent job assimilating immigrants into our culture. We had to. We were (and still are) a nation of immigrants. Because we did such a good job in the past, we avoided many of the troubles that affect other nations, like ethnic and religious civil war. Today, however, we are replacing the notion of assimilation with the more politically correct concept of "multiculturalism."

Multiculturalism is the notion that we don't need to assimilate new members of our society. Instead, we should change to accommodate them. It is also the idea that we should teach immigrants in their native tongue rather than in English. It is the idea that all cultural values are equally acceptable and serves as an educational manifestation of moral relativism. Advocates of multiculturalism believe that hysterical criticism of our own country is appropriate, but any criticism of others, is racist. I hope these people will move to Yugoslavia.

What is truly terrifying, however, is that most of the people who think this way run our schools from top to bottom. Multiculturalism is imposed upon our students relentlessly from elementary school to college. Most textbook and curriculum companies have "sensitivity committees" that filter out any "culturally offensive" material regardless of historical fact. In fact, a local Washington school district banned Halloween because it might be offensive to Wiccans (That's witches for those of you who failed your last PC test).

When students get to high school they must navigate the test we call the WASL. In some ways, the curriculum preparing students for this test is an Orwellian indoctrination tool masquerading as homework. Students are forced to adopt a normative stance that conforms to current multicultural fads in order to pass. If they do pass, they attend one of our universities where multiculturalism is worshiped with an uncompromising intensity that rivals zealotry. Worse yet, the most fervent practitioners of multiculturalism infest our schools of education … which produce the next crop of teachers … and the cycle continues.

We have spent so much of the last generation convincing ourselves that we need to respect the cultures of others, we forgot to demand that immigrants reciprocate in kind. I will respect the cultural eccentricities of immigrants when they agree to respect the culture of the nation they are migrating to. Or, if nothing else, at least agree not to burn down the cities of their new host nation. I guess a welfare check and free medical care isn't enough anymore.

Isn't it ironic that we call the Minutemen who guard our borders "vigilantes" but we refer to advocates of multiculturalism and open borders "progressive"? There has to be a middle ground. We don't want jingoism to be part of the education process, but we do have a responsibility to teach children our culture, history, and yes, our values. If necessary, we need to ensure that immigrants are assimilated into our culture as a prerequisite for admission. I know some of you will have a field day writing passionate letters to the editor calling me a racist or suggesting I'm xenophobic. Have at it. But I have three replies before you even write them.

Paris is burning. Paris is burning. Paris is burning.

◆   ◆   ◆

And write letters they did! I had besmirched the sacred cow of academia: the blind worship of multiculturalism. If I had walked into a National Rifle Association meeting with a Jane Fonda button on my chest, I could not have hit a more sensitive nerve. I had the head of the "Diversity Center" write a letter. I had the Education professors write in. I had history professors and the like all calling me names. In the course of the letters that came in, it was suggested that I approve of genocide, was a blatant racist, and wanted minorities walled away in ghettoes. Of course, none of those accusations could be further from the mark, but it was graduate school all over again. The Left was resorting back to their favorite approach. If you don't like what someone has said, just call them a racist. It's easier than thinking.

In one of the rare instances where I wrote a column in response to my critics, I addressed their complaints the following month. Because the people who wrote those letters are still around, I have changed their real names to something generic. Looking back at my reply, it was one of the few times I let my anger get the better of me. My response was pretty biting.

◆   ◆   ◆

"Paris is Burning: A Response to the Critics"

Well, well, well. It looks like I touched a nerve last month, huh? In my November column I noted that most academics worship "multiculturalism" with a "cult-like intensity." And, as if they were eager to prove me right, many of my university brethren wrote into the *Daily Record* with responses that ranged from the misguided to the offensive. I could let the subject drop, but I never walk away from a fight, and this is a good fight, one worth having.

Mr. "Smith", from our "Diversity Center" got the ball rolling. He suggests those who oppose multiculturalism and "E Pluribus Unum" advocate genocide, internment, slavery, and segregation. In academia, we call this "setting up a straw man." The fallacy is committed when a person simply ignores a person's actual position and substitutes a distorted version of his own. Of course people who prefer a culture of consensus do not promote the abhorrent acts Mr. Smith describes and I suspect he knows this. Silly rhetoric aside, he completely missed the point. Yes, the United States has committed terrible acts in its history. We did commit genocide on Native Americans. We did enslave Africans. But, why don't Native Americans strap dynamite to their chest and kill innocent civilians? Why do African-Americans still consider themselves Americans? Why don't they demand an autonomous political region? Why is it that the US has never suffered IRA-like attacks from within? Other nations have committed crimes similar to the US. But these other countries seem trapped in continual cycles of violence, while the US is not. Why is it that minority groups that have suffered at the hands of the US do not behave the same way as abused minority groups in other nations? The answer is cultural assimilation or "political socialization." Despite our historic tragedies, our cultural assimilation has been able to partially heal the wounds of racial, ethnic, and religious divisions. France has not. Yugoslavia did not.

The arguments of Professor "Jones" are almost too embarrassing to respond to, but ignorance left uncorrected has a tendency to become "conventional wisdom." Mr. Jones contends "multiculturalism is the notion we should not be racist ..." Yes, that is one definition.... if you have a junior high reading level. But multiculturalism encompasses more than that simplistic credo. He goes on to suggest that opposition to multiculturalism is racist. I predicted in my last column that the intellectually inept would resort to name-calling. In my line of work, if you can't come up with an intelligent argument you just call someone a racist, sexist, or homophobe. It's easier than thinking. But Mr. Jones' comments turn from embarrassing to offensive when he suggest that we "should let Paris burn" until there is "justice." To the women who were dragged off of busses and beaten, I'm sure his comments are comforting. Under Jones' rationale, any terrorist with a social justice gripe is completely within his rights to blow up a plane, suicide bomb a bus, or drop anthrax in the water supply. It's strange that someone so "progressive" has a philosophy closer to bin Laden than Martin Luther King Jr. It's more stunning that someone who would make such a comment has the nerve to call anyone else a racist.

Professor "Miller", at least, had a better definition of multiculturalism. He noted, "[it] is the belief that no single ethnic, linguistic, or religious identity should dominate over another." Where he goes astray is in describing the effects of multiculturalism. He contends that it "encourages racial and ethnic harmony and discourages ghettoization, hatred, and violence." I wish it did. But the exact opposite is true. Multiculturalism IS ghettoization! It says to students, "focus on what makes you different." The reason that Irish-, Italian-, and German-Americans all get along so well today is because the children of those immigrants chose not to focus on their old identities and differences, but instead blend into their new culture. As a result, we don't even use the term German-American anymore. It's become outdated. When my great-grandparents came to America they spoke only German and insisted they were German-Americans. But my grandparents spoke fluent English and considered themselves simply Americans. No one interned them. No one enslaved them. No one subjected them to violence. They assimilated and I'm better off for it. Thanks Grandma! What makes assimilation so difficult today is that children of recent immigrants want to blend into their new culture, but we have educators telling them to focus on what separates us. In the end, multiculturalism is like picking at the scab of a wound, making sure it never heals.

Professor "Johnson" contends that America has always been a multicultural nation and therefore multiculturalism is necessary. Again, exactly backwards. It is only multicultural nations, like the US, that need to build institutions of cultural assimilation. Cultural assimilation in a unitary culture is a lot like the sound of one hand clapping.

The most painful part of this debate is the knowledge that the academics who push multiculturalism sincerely believe that they are making the world a better place, just like Chamberlain sincerely thought he was promoting peace in 1939.

◆   ◆   ◆

There is a funny addendum to the column about Muslim immigration to France. Right about the time this article was making the rounds, my wife and I decided to buy some land out in the country. We found a nice three-acre parcel overlooking Mt. Rainer. The guy that sold it to us was a long time hay and oat farmer and all of his neighbors were farmers too. They were not happy he had sold a parcel to "one of those liberal University folk." It was like "There goes the neighborhood." He was getting phone calls asking him, "How could you?" Then my article came out.

His neighbors stopped bothering him and told him, "He's okay. He can build a house out here, but no one else from down there." It's strange being a conservative political science professor. The liberals you work with think you are a little off in the head and the conservative farmers you hang out with are pretty sure that if you work at a university long enough your colleagues will corrupt you. Oh well, I am a man without a place in the world. The life of a heretic I guess.

I have two more columns I want to share. Both about the French. They're just such an easy target, sometimes I can't resist. It's like Rosie O'Donnell with a handful of darts in a room with nothing but Donald Trump pictures. I just can't help myself. To be fair to the French, I'm going to end on a positive note, but not quite yet.

To say that the French have never been good at economics is an understatement. It's a country where ideology trumps rationality. Usually what saves a country from bad economic policy are the negative consequences that result from bad economic policy. For example, if you have a government that adopts policies that encourage inflation, then usually people start suffering from inflation and demand a change in policy at the polls. Not always true in France. They have bad economic policy and typically just keep making things worse. Kind of like Limburger cheese.

One of the worst policies the French have is that it is very difficult to fire anyone in France. Sounds good on the surface, but ask anyone who has ever run a business: if you can't fire people, you won't hire people. It's just that simple. At the time I wrote "French Stupidity Strikes Again" the French government was finally beginning to see the error of their ways. The ruling government was introducing new laws that would actually make it legal for an employer to fire someone if they didn't come to work. How radical. How capitalist. Unfortunately, the law didn't go anywhere. A combination of stupidity on the part of French voters and the temerity on the part of French leaders scuttled the bill. But there was an upside. I had something to write about in my column that month.

◆   ◆   ◆

"French Stupidity Strikes Again!"

Thank God for the French. Every time I turn on the news and see Americans doing something ridiculous (rejecting port deals, encouraging illegal immigration, firing employees who don't join unions) I am comforted by the fact that no matter what we do, the French will always be able to top us in a stupidity competition.

France has one of the highest unemployment rates in the free world—hovering around 10-14%. If the US had unemployment rates like that, we would call it a depression. And the French can't blame their high unemployment rate on cyclical factors; their unemployment is chronic. The picture is far worse for low-skilled workers between the ages of 16-24. Their unemployment rates range from 28-39%. In contrast, the American economy is adding hundred of thousands of new jobs every month. We are at historic lows when it comes to unemployment. Thank you Mr. Bush and your tax cuts.

France, on the other hand, has stunningly high unemployment rates because they regulate their labor markets so excessively. They have high minimum wages, cushy unemployment benefits, and of course the policy that has been making all the headlines this month—it is almost impossible to fire a French worker after he has been hired. Basically, they have labor laws similar to what the US would have if the Democratic Party was in charge.

Uncharacteristically, the French government actually tried to do something intelligent this month. They sought to repeal the law that made it so difficult to fire younger workers. This would have been an excellent leap forward for French employees. Believe it or not, the more regulations a nation has preventing employers from firing people, the higher the jobless rate. Simply put, governments that seek to protect employment with labor restrictions actually cause more unemployment. This happens because when employers know they cannot fire a worker they are less likely to hire a worker. Here is an analogy. How many of you would be willing to go on a blind date, if, after that one date, you could never break up with them? I didn't think so.

The French need to understand that economies go up and go down. When they go up, businesses hire people. When the economy goes down, they let people go. However, if an employer knows that he will not be able to reduce the work force in bad times, they are unwilling to increase the work force in good times. I used to teach this to high school students and they got it. Why can't the French?

France is finally learning this lesson. They are learning it from their neighbors in Ireland. In the last decade Ireland has moved towards more Thatcher/ Reaganesque labor and economic policies. As a result, Ireland has the lowest unemployment rate in Europe. They learned that if employers are allowed to fire people they are also willing to hire them. Of course, large infusions of cash from the European Union didn't hurt, but that is a column for another day.

The ironic part of this story is that the young workers of France are taking to the streets fighting this new law. Unbelievable. For the first time in decades the French government is doing something right and the very people they are trying help are the ones fighting them so intently.

This is the danger of economic ignorance. What you don't know can hurt you. There will always be those people who think with their hearts instead of their brain. They will tell you that minimum wage laws help workers. They will tell you making it difficult for employers to fire people saves jobs. They will tell you the Department of Labor and Industries helps workers. In reality, the people who push these policies do more harm to workers than any employer could ever do.

All of these policies just lead to higher unemployment, a lower standard of living, and a large pool of disaffected young people with nothing to do but riot in the streets.

◆   ◆   ◆

With all this French bashing, I should end on a positive note. Finally, after years of pathetic economic growth, the French people had had enough. A government can only sell the dream of socialist utopia so long before citizens start asking when the utopia is going to be there. In 2007, the French got sick of waiting. A man by the name of Nicolas Sarkozy emerged onto the French political scene draped in the rhetoric of Margaret Thatcher and Ronald Reagan. He actually went to the French electorate and told them, "We need to be more like Americans." It was a statement I never thought I would hear in my lifetime. If Charles De Gaulle had been alive that comment would have killed him.

He told the French the truth. He said if they wanted prosperity, they would have to work for it. If they wanted wealth, the size of government would have to shrink. Entrepreneurs would have to take risks, even fail from time to time. He was telling the French what everyone in America (at least those in the Republican Party) already knew. Success doesn't come easy and people create wealth, not governments. And much to my surprise, the French decided to give it a try. Sarkozy won. Not a landslide, but he won. Now history waits for the results. Will he hold firm like Thatcher and Reagan? Or will he fold under the pressure of riots, unions, and civil service workers?

One thing is for sure. If Mr. Sarkozy wants Muslim immigrants to stop burning down his cities, he has two options. He can put up a big wall on the French border, maybe something more effective than the Maginot line, or he can build up his economy. If history is a guide, dollars work better than walls.

◆   ◆   ◆

"France Finally Sees the Light"

And so, one of the last dominos falls. France, long the stubborn adherent to "companionate socialism" and "egalitarianism," has finally accepted the utter failure of a demeaning economic system. It took a few generations, but even the intractable French came to realize there is nothing compassionate about a social state that leaves 20% of its people without jobs, creates a society with no social mobility, and demoralizes an underclass with no hope of advancement. They realized that the only thing egalitarian about the French system was that it left everyone equally miserable and poor. The French wanted to be the socialist model for Europe but realized you can't be the model for anything if no one is following.

To borrow a phrase, "their long national nightmare is finally over." 85% of the French electorate went to the polls last week and elected an unabashedly pro-American, free-marketer in the form of Nicolas Sarkozy. Sarkozy has promised to undo France's entrepreneurial strangling policies such as the 35-hour work week, confiscatory tax rates, and incentive killing social welfare benefits. In France, tax rates are so high that anyone with a good idea or a marginal work-ethic leaves the country, draining the nation of jobs and tax revenue. The social welfare benefits are so high that anyone out of work would be silly to actually look for a job. The civil service unions are so powerful that a French bureaucrat can be as incompetent as an American bureaucrat and still never lose their job.

Well, the gravy train is over. Not necessarily due to a change of heart, but because the gravy bowl is empty. A nation can only sustain those policies so long before they go bankrupt. That day has come for the French. Now Sarkozy must follow in the footsteps of the British, Americans, Germans, and most recently the Irish. Each of these nations flirted with socialism and came to realize its failures. Margaret Thatcher had to wean her people from the dependency a welfare state creates. Ronald Reagan had to remind the American people that wealth comes from work, not government. And recently, the Irish have come to remind "old Europe" that free markets and free people are the best way to drag a country out of economic malaise.

I have always believed that, in the long run, good ideas drive out bad ideas. The reason I believe this is that ultimately, ideas are not judged by the ideology behind them, but by the results they produce. The ideologue can only preach at the pulpit so long before people go outside and see what they have wrought. Sometimes that can be a long journey. It took the Russians 80 years, the Chinese 50 years, but British only 20. All in all the battle of ideas has been fought and won. Egalitarianism and socialism have lost and are now reputable only in North Korea, Cuba, American universities and the backwaters of the Democratic Party.

Earlier this year, I noted the passing of Milton Freidman, the famous Chicago School economist. I think that on this day, he is looking down on France and smiling for the first time.

The lesson for Americans in this French story is that the price of liberty is the eternal vigilance of its people. Reagan reminded us that liberty is so fragile because it can be lost in a single generation. Despite 200 years of pursuing free markets, free trade, and free people, there will always be people like Hillary Clinton who want us to trade all that for the illusion of "economic equality." I was reminded of this fact when recently speaking with a group of Russian exchange students on the CWU campus. They were shocked at how many American politicians were calling for state-run medical systems, paid family leave, and more control of the economy. One of them said to me, "Don't Americans know what happened to us in the Soviet Union? We can tell them how bad it was. They should come and talk to us." Yes they should Vadim. Yes they should.

7

Public Policy

Public policy is complex for several reasons. For starters, what is intuitively correct doesn't always work in the real world. Take the minimum wage for example. If the government increases the minimum wage, people will make more money.... right? Not really. It sounds simple and straight forward, but it isn't. In reality, an increase in the minimum wage causes an increase in both inflation and unemployment. As labor becomes more expensive, employers "buy" less of it. As the cost of labor goes up, the prices for products must go up to pay for it. In the end, we are no better off than when we started.

The problem we face as a society is that most voters don't have the time to engage in the complex analysis of public policy options. Most of us are limited to: a higher wage sounds like more money to me.... I'm for it. Much of what political commentators such as myself, and elected officials do all day, is try to explain how our gut reactions to policy ideas are not always correct.

Another difficulty with public policy is that sometimes what works in the real world doesn't mesh with our ideology. That is a tough one to swallow for many partisans. Not all tax increases result in job losses. That's hard to admit if you are a strong Republican. Welfare reform worked. That is difficult to swallow if you are a strong Democrat. But good public policy making includes the ability, nay the necessity, to admit when you are wrong. Hard for anyone to do. Almost impossible for most politicians.

And finally, there is the "law of unintended consequences." Many public policy makers think in a linier and finite fashion. Law A will fix Problem B. It rarely works that way. Law A sometimes fixes Problem B. But just as often, Law A causes people to react so that they can avoid the consequences of Law A. We call these "unintended consequences." To use our minimum wage example again, if a lawmaker wants to fix problem B (low wages) with Law A that increases the minimum wage, he may just force businesses on the Washington border to move to Oregon and Idaho instead. Oops. That would be an unintended consequence. The problem for policy makers is that people are not pawns. People don't just move the way lawmakers want us to. Often, we move of our own accord and for our own interests.

The problem of unintended consequences is so fundamental to the public policy process that I want to start this chapter with it. But first a little background. I live in a rural area of the country that, like many small communities with beautiful landscapes, is experiencing rapid growth. That means change; and change always brings with it political angst. Many environmentalists in my county are decrying all the home building that is taking place on the hillsides and one-time farm land. Who is to blame for this change? Evil developers? Corrupt county commissioners? Someone must be responsible for allowing our county to change from a quaint rural community to a bustling suburb. In my article, "The Law of Unintended Consequences" I found a different culprit—the very environmentalists who where complaining about the growth. I charged that their earlier policies had the unintended effect of causing the very residential growth they were complaining about.

◆   ◆   ◆

"The Law of Unintended Consequences"

Many rural communities in Washington are experiencing rapid residential growth. Homes are intruding on traditional farm land and once vacant hillsides are becoming dotted with homes. For understandable reasons, this disturbs many people. Growth has led many activists to call for zoning moratoriums or other restrictions on development. Unfortunately, many voters and especially many policy makers have failed to grasp the counterintuitive notion that, sometimes, laws designed to protect rural areas actually backfire and cause additional development. Because this topic is capturing so much political attention, it's a good time to discuss The Law of Unintended Consequences. The "Law" tells us that when people set out to accomplish Objective A by imposing Rule B they may, indeed, accomplish Objective A, but they may also create Unintended Consequence C. This is exactly what is happening across the state and it is why the "rural nature" of our state isn't what it once was.

There are three industries that make parts of our state rural: farming and agriculture, ranching, and logging. With these industries come open spaces, recreational forests, and beautiful views. Without them, we get subdivisions. The dilemma we have been facing in the last three decades is that the very industries that make communities rural are also industries that have potentially harmful effects on the environment. In our zeal to protect the environment (Objective A) we imposed a cumbersome host of regulations on rural industries (Rule B). We have, as intended, created a more protected environment.

Unfortunately, we have also increased the cost of doing business in these three industries, pushing many farmers, ranchers and loggers to "exit the market." When they exit the market, they have large plats of land they can no longer use and so begin selling their land to developers (Unintended Consequence C).

Take for example the now gone logging industry in Kittitas County. When it existed, people enjoyed scenic views, hiking and fishing in the summer and snowmobiling in the winter. But, there was also concern about logging's impact on the environment. To alleviate concerns about the environment, our logging industry came under a well-intentioned assault. A 1998 lawsuit by the Alpine Lakes Protection Society against Plum Creek Logging shows the extent to which we now regulate logging in this state.

When Plum Creek actually tried to log some of its trees (you know, to stay in business) the company was regulated by the Department of Natural Resources, the Department of Ecology, and the Forest Practices Board. It was also subject to the State Environmental Policy Act (SEPA), the Endangered Species Act, and Watershed Analysis requirements.

But that wasn't enough. When Plum Creek was sued, it had to prove it was mitigating effects on recreation, aesthetics, and grizzly bears. As noble as these goals are, the costly rules have the unintended consequence of making logging very difficult and unprofitable. When the logging became unprofitable, the logging company had to sell its land. Hmmm? Who would want to buy large tracks of forestland in a rural county close to Seattle? In step the developers.

This story can be repeated for both farmers and ranchers. Those on the left correctly point out that farmer's use of pesticides and cows harm river banks and riparian zones. So, the state regulates and regulates to the benefit of the environment. But, these regulations make it very difficult and expensive to use the land.

Many farmers and ranchers eventually throw up their hands, and realize it is easier to sell than navigate increasingly complex regulations enforced by a compassionless Department of Ecology.

If a farmer loses the ability to farm, he is not going to leave the land untouched for your viewing pleasure. He is going to sell the land to a developer. The Law of Unintended Consequences strikes again. Laws designed to protect the environment actually end up encouraging the spread of subdivisions.

Here is the irony. Activists who once crusaded against loggers, ranchers and farmers are now the same people who are expressing shock over the decreasing rural nature of Washington State. Refusing to accept they are the cause of this long-term change, they seek an easy scapegoat. The simplistic blame developers. The ignorant blame inattentive county commissioners, and the clueless blame free trade.

Here is the uncomfortable truth: shuffling county commissioners, re-writing the Growth Management Act, or amending local Comprehensive Plans will have limited impact on preserving rural communities, unless we also adopt a regulatory environment that is friendly to the professions that make our state rural in the first place. Too many people believe that salvation can be found in a clever zoning plan or a mandatory building moratorium. Such people are misled by the mistaken belief that we are running out of farm or ranchland, when in reality we are simply running out of farmers and ranchers.

◆   ◆   ◆

"The Law of Unintended Consequences" was one of the few articles I have written that attracted statewide attention. Written as an op-ed piece for the Washington Policy Center, it was disseminated across the state to many media outlets. It even made its way to the floor of the Washington Legislature. A few months after I wrote it, I had an ex-student call me. He was working as a Legislative Assistant in the House and told me that he was handed a copy of my article at a briefing he attended. Made me feel good. I never know if anything that I write has any effect. I don't know if this article did either, but at least a few policy makers read it. Maybe that is good enough.

Other parts of policy making don't make me feel so good. Nothing makes me angrier than when people use the democratic process to take things (land, money, property) from other people just because they have a majority. I call this the "dark underside of democracy." In general, most Americans have a positive view of democracy. It is rule by the people and that sounds good. But democracy is not rule by the people. Democracy is rule by 51 percent of the people. Unfortunately, that means that 51 percent of the people can take just about anything they want from the other 49 percent of the people. Our Framers tried to create a system that limited the ability of majorities to take whatever they wanted from hapless minorities. Most of it you can find it in the Bill of Rights. But the Bill of Rights was written BEFORE we invented income taxes. The Framers never thought to protect our money from greedy majorities because they didn't think our money was at risk. Oh how wrong they were.

In "Celebrating Thankstaking" I tried to explain the inherent dangers of democracy. I wrote it in November just after the people of Washington, or I should say, large majorities in Washington exercised their vote to take other people's money and land in the 2006 elections. Initiative 933 was a bill that would have required the state to pay landowners if the state seized their land or by regulation, made the land worthless. It failed. Initiative 920 wanted to eliminate the estate tax. It also failed. In both cases, small minorities (farmers with land and elderly with large assets) were trying to protect themselves from majorities that wanted to take what they had. Both minority groups lost.

◆   ◆   ◆

"Celebrating Thankstaking"

Last Thursday, everyone in Washington celebrated Thanksgiving. On Election Day, two weeks earlier, a little more than half of Washingtonians celebrated "Thanks-taking." This lesser known holiday occurs every two years when majorities, using the process known as democracy, take whatever they want from helpless minorities. Two majority populations got to celebrate this year. Those without land celebrated by voting to take land from those who do have it; and those who do not plan to pass on assets to their children celebrated by voting to take the money of those who were planning on it.

America's celebration of this ignoble holiday dates back to a time right after the Revolution but before the drafting of the Constitution. In the 1780s a large group of Pennsylvania farmers were highly indebted to a small group of Philadelphia bankers. Rather than pay back the loans, the farmers, who represented a much larger portion of the population, simply voted to eliminate their financial obligations. This blatant act of "majority tyranny" was not lost on James Madison. He understood that the bane of all democracies is that majorities can vote to take the property, resources, or even the civil liberties of any minority group. For this reason, Madison carefully balanced within the Constitution majority power and minority rights. Although majorities were given significant powers in Article I of the Constitution, those powers were checked by minority protections in the Bill of Rights.

Unfortunately for modern Americans, Madison focused solely on political oppression, and ignored economic oppression. To Madison, this made sense. His Constitution only authorized majorities to engage in the political realm. The federal government did not have the power to tax income, so he saw no need to craft minority protections against redistributive policies. A century later, Americans saw fit to amend the Constitution by giving the government the power to tax income. Their fatal flaw was that while granting the majority the right to levy taxes, they failed to grant minorities any protection from this power. Ever since 1913, Americans have been able to vote themselves the resources of other people as long as those "other people" represented a minority of the populace. We've been celebrating "Thanks-taking" ever since.

Two weeks ago, the tradition was in full force. Both I-933 and I-920 were attempts by minorities to protect themselves from selfish and indifferent majorities. In both cases, the majorities of Washington said "no."

In the case of I-933, minority landowners pleaded with our citizens to "stop taking our land, but if you insist on doing so, please at least pay us for it." But a majority of voters in this state (especially the Westside) live in apartments, condos, or suburban house lots. Their response was, "No. We can take whatever we want, whenever we want, and we don't have to pay you anything because we outnumber you." Welcome to Democracy 101. This callous attitude (which is the root of slavery throughout history) may be selfish, but it is also rational. As shoppers, would you pay for your groceries if, instead, you could just vote to take them home for free?

I-920 pitted an even smaller minority against an overwhelming majority. Those who have built up considerable assets to pass onto their children are an extreme minority. It didn't take long for a clever politician to say "hey, let's take those peoples' money and give it to our kids' education." By a simple vote, many people chose to take what was not theirs and give it to themselves. The majorities who voted against I-920 rationalized their theft by noting they were helping education and only a few people were affected. I hope these people don't raise children. Can you imagine a parent telling their child it is OK to steal if you only steal from a few people and you steal for a "good cause?" This Robin Hood rational overlooks one simple fact: despite all his good intentions, Robin Hood was just a thief. If you voted against I-920 … so are you. You took something that wasn't yours and using a ballot box instead of a gun doesn't make you any less guilty.

◆   ◆   ◆

Sometimes, I just love to predict the future. I probably shouldn't do that in a book. Some student of mine is going to dig this thing up years from now, bring it to class, and call me on all the things I got wrong. But damn the torpedoes, full speed ahead.

My prediction is that decades from now we will look back at 2005 as one of the great missed opportunities in political history. For fifty years, Social Security has been "the third rail of politics," which is a fancy way of saying it's untouchable. Any politician who messes with it seals his own fate. It doesn't matter that the system is going broke and that there is little chance I will get my money back when I retire. Touch Social Security and you commit political suicide.

Until President Bush. He has been one of the only politicians in my lifetime to be honest about Social Security. He told the American people straight out that the system cannot sustain itself under its current design. We are living longer. The Baby Boom generation is retiring and there are fewer workers per retiree than there were a decade ago. We are running a 1930s system in a 2000 world. Something's gotta give.

In 2005, with majorities in both houses of Congress, Bush put a plan on the table to allow people to invest 5 percent of their Social Security taxes in private accounts. A great idea, but a complicated idea. And complicated ideas are easy to demonize.

Democrats did just that. By the end of the debate about modernizing Social Security for the 21st Century, demagoguery had won the day. Democrats had people believing that all your money was going to go to Enron; Grandma and Grandpa were going to starve when they retired; and that we common citizens were way too stupid to invest our own money. It worked. Social Security reform went down in flames. In politics, if you can't out-think your opponent, out-scare your opponent.

The day is coming when we are going to regret that. You can only take more water out of a lake than you put in for so long. Then the lake goes dry. Our lake is going dry fast. In a few decades there are going to be lots of people retiring and there won't be Social Security checks coming. When that happens a lot of self-righteous pundits are gong to pound the table on Sunday talk shows and ask WHY no one did anything about a disaster EVERYONE saw coming. I'll be old that day. But I will speak up and say, "Not everyone did nothing." President Bush tried, he just got beat.

During the great Social Security debate, I weighed in. I tried to make the complex simple in "The Social Security Debate: The Forgotten Variable."

◆   ◆   ◆

"The Social Security Debate: The Forgotten Variable"

There is a reason Harry Truman was always looking for a "one-handed economist." Sometimes, economics is counterintuitive and at other times, downright contradictory. Take for instance the need for personal savings and personal spending. As any good Keynesian knows, the key to economic growth is consumer spending. If you leave that dollar in the cookie jar, money becomes stationary and people lose their jobs. True enough Mr. Keynes. But as all good economists also know, the rate of economic growth is a function of a nation's savings rate. Businesses need money to borrow for plant expansion and to invest in better technology. From this perspective: a dollar saved today becomes two dollars spent tomorrow.

This cumbersome introduction leads me to this week's topic, or what I like to call "the forgotten variable" in the Social Security reform debate. In today's partisan atmosphere, or what might be termed "the politics of instant gratification" we are losing sight of one of the most important arguments in the Social Security debate. Changing the way we run the Social Security system will go a long way towards changing the way Americans save. Before the advent of the Social Security system, every American knew that he or she had to put away a little money each month to save for retirement. This money went into banks where other people (small business owners, farmers, and industrialists) would borrow it to modernize plants or expand family owned businesses. With plenty of entrepreneurial capital available, interest rates remained low and economic growth continued to improve our standard of living.

But after we implemented our current Social Security system, the incentive to save diminished. Americans knew that come that 62nd or 65th birthday, the US government was going to pony-up and provide a check for as long as you lived. Therefore, why not spend every dime that came home via that paycheck. As of today, the US has one of the lowest savings rates in the world. According to the Bureau of Economic Analysis the US savings rate in 2001 was 1.5% and has hovered below 10% for the last six decades.

But what about all that money the FICA monster takes out of my check each month? Isn't that money saved away somewhere until I retire? No. It isn't. That money goes directly to elderly citizens drawing Social Security. And therein lies the rub. The 6.2% that comes out of your check each month does not go into savings. It is immediately spent by current retirees. None of that money goes to banks to loan out. None of it is used to modernize our technology or increase the pool of productive capital.

Now imagine if instead of simply transferring money from young worker A to old retiree B, young worker A actually saved $500,000 over his lifetime. He invested in bonds, stocks, or just plain savings. All that money would sit there for 50 years, being used by industrious, inventive Americans. According to Harvard economist Martin Feldstein, if the United States were to adopt some form of private accounts, we would increase the overall pool of personal savings by 10 trillion dollars. Yes, folks, that was trillion with a "t". With such a massive increase in available investment capital, interest rates would plummet. Economic growth would skyrocket.

Unfortunately, the debate about Social Security reform has largely ignored substantive economic issues. In politics there is a version of Gresham's Law where
superficial political debate crowds out substantive debate. With buzzwords like
"privatization" and "benefit cuts" floating around, it's hard to focus on the boring
nuts and bolts of Social Security reform.

So what is the real reason the Democratic Party opposes personal accounts? It's
not the numbers. Believe it or not, Democrats can add just as well as Republicans. The problem for Democrats is that if we tackle the Social Security problem
today, there are lots of long term options: personal accounts, benefit cuts, tax
increases, means testing, payment indexing, and more. But, if we wait until 2040
to fix the problem, there are only two short term options: benefit cuts or tax
increases. Which is exactly what Democrats want. Their preferred solution is to
increase the payroll tax that funds Social Security. But they need a crisis situation
to push through such a policy. By waiting 35 more years, pushing the system to
bankruptcy, they will be able to justify an "emergency tax increase" to "save"
Social Security. For Democrats, it's too early to save Social Security. They need
to wait until the only option that will work is the option they most desire. And
you guessed it. For Democrats, the solution to every problem is a tax increase.

◆   ◆   ◆

When I was a kid, my dad told me that whenever I was a guest at someone else's
house, I should never talk about religion or politics at the dinner table. Advice I
followed until I was middle-aged. When I got asked to speak at a Unitarian
Church by one of the town's leading liberals and the topic was abortion politics, I
was thinking of my dad that day. I often look back and wonder how I ended up
at a podium in a church, talking about abortion … to a bunch of liberals.

If you haven't been to a Unitarian church service, I should tell you they are a little
different than a typical "sermon." They are very informal. They usually invite a
speaker, but the topic doesn't have to be religion. And most of their members are
very liberal, politically speaking. In fact, the Unitarian Church is open to atheists.
In some ways, it's more of a Sunday spiritual meeting group than a formal church
service.

One day I got a call. They wanted me to come speak at their Sunday service. I
was caught a little off guard. As a political scientist I get asked to speak all the

time, but usually at a conference or an association meeting. Never a church. I know my Bible, but I don't know it well enough to sermonize from the pulpit. What exactly would you like me to speak about, I asked.

They asked me to speak about how the appointment of Samuel Alito to the Supreme Court will affect Roe v. Wade. Now I have to tell you that the lady who asked me to speak is one of the nicest ladies you will ever meet. But I kind of just stared at her. You want me, the most well-known Republican in the county to talk about abortion politics.... in a church ... to a bunch of Democrats? Sure. Why not?

Turns out, they were just as wary as I was. The woman who asked me to speak was one of two people responsible for setting up guest speakers at her church. When her partner found out she had approached me to speak, he told her she was on her own, and he didn't want his name associated with the program at all. Which was kind of weird since her partner was also her husband. Ouch. Tough crowd.

In the end, it was one of the most enjoyable Sundays my wife and I have ever spent at church. Much to the congregation's surprise, I told them that overturning *Roe v. Wade* would have little or no effect on abortion in the United States. When I tell my conservative friends the same thing, they are equally shocked. Shocked or not, it's true.

My talk was based on an article I had published about a year earlier before Justice Rehnquist had died. At the time, the Senate was voting on whether to eliminate the filibuster to stop Democrats from blocking President Bush's judicial appointment. But, like most all things that intersect with judicial politics, it was more about abortion than the filibuster.

◆   ◆   ◆

"Misunderstanding Roe v. Wade"

As the Senate gears up for one of its biggest fights in memory by considering whether to eliminate the filibuster, I thought it would be helpful to use this month's column to reflect on the historical roots of this debate. Like most fights in the judicial arena the culprit in this case is *Roe v. Wade* (1973). It has been more than 30 years since *Roe* was decided, but the consequences continue to echo through current political fights.

One reason judicial confirmation fights have been so intense in the past few years is that the tenuous equilibrium on the Supreme Court supporting abortion rights is in danger of being disrupted. If Chief Justice Rehnquist retires, or 85-year-old Justice Stevens leaves for any reason, President Bush will get to nominate two (or even three) new justices. Such a seismic change in the Court's makeup would put abortion law back in play and possibly lead to the overturning of *Roe*.

For people who support abortion rights, such a development seems to be an impending disaster. For people who oppose abortion, such a development looks like the realization of a political dream. The reality is that neither of these interpretations is correct. Both sides of the abortion debate fundamentally misunderstand the legal nature of the *Roe v. Wade* decision and therefore fundamentally misunderstand the impact overturning the decision will have on abortion law.

Prior to *Roe,* each state legislature decided whether abortion would be legal or not. As a result, abortion was already legal in many states long before *Roe* was decided. Texas happened to be one state where it was not legal. When *Roe v. Wade* was handed down, the Court determined that the Texas abortion statute was illegal. Because the Supreme Court is a national court, the decision also had the effect of overturning all the other restrictive abortion statutes in any state still prohibiting abortion.

Roe did not make abortion legal, it made it illegal for states to prohibit it. It may sound like wordplay, but this nuance is very important. The repeal of *Roe* will not automatically make abortion illegal. It will simply, once again, empower state legislatures around the country to decide whether abortion should be completely legal, completely illegal, or some compromise in between.

For example, if *Roe* is overturned, abortion is going to remain perfectly legal in Massachusetts. The day after *Roe* is overturned, the state legislature there will legalize abortion on a simple voice vote. However, in Utah, it is very likely that abortion will promptly become illegal. Earlier studies examining the question "which states will keep abortion legal after Roe is overturned?" have had different results. According to the Center for Reproductive Rights, an abortion rights advocacy group, without *Roe*, 30 states would likely outlaw abortion. A Naral Pro-Choice America study puts the number at only 12. Only a few states have "trigger laws" which have language automatically reinstating abortion restrictions the day after *Roe* is overturned.

The larger lesson here is that overturning *Roe* is not the "end all. be all" of abortion politics. Both sides of the issue have made *Roe* either their Holy Grail or sacred cow. It is neither. Overturning *Roe* will be just the beginning of a larger fight that will move from the courts to the state legislatures. Given that abortion is a moral issue, and not really a constitutional issue (there is no right to privacy in the Constitution despite what some people will tell you), it probably belongs to the democratic process in state legislatures. By making state legislatures decide abortion law, two things will happen. When an elected official states that he/she is pro-life or pro-choice it will actually be more than demagogic rhetoric. That representative will have to match his vote with his campaign. Secondly, the courts will be free to once again start interpreting democratically= enacted law instead of drafting law based on their personal value systems. When that happens, all this fighting about who gets confirmed will go away.

◆   ◆   ◆

One of the few issues that ranks up there on the "controversy meter" as high as abortion is illegal immigration. If you live in a rural farming town, that goes double. I tried to stay out of this debate for a long time. I have a lot of friends who are farmers and orchardists. They tell me flat out that if they can't use labor from Mexico, they will go out of business. On the other hand, laws are laws and we don't get to pick and choose which ones to follow. A nation has a right to protect its borders. Period.

But I can only stand so much. When I saw students in Los Angeles taking down American flags and putting up Mexican flags, I was done standing on the sidelines. When Mexican President Vicente Fox went on TV criticizing the United States because he didn't like the way we treated his citizens, I threw something at the TV. When I saw thousands of illegal immigrants "demanding" their "rights" in marches across America, I sat down at my computer.

I also looked up Mexico's immigration laws. Their hypocrisy is appalling.

◆   ◆   ◆

"Mexico.… Heal Thyself"

I have come to the conclusion that the Mexican people and the Mexican government understand immigration issues far better than the American people and our government. In fact, the Mexican people and its leadership are so confident about their grasp of immigration policy that they feel comfortable coming to our country to tell us how things should be done. President Vicente Fox berated the US Congress over its bills to clamp down on illegal immigration and criticized the Minutemen for watching the border. Thousands of illegal immigrants took to our streets demanding their "rights". Because these people seem so confident in their knowledge of immigration policy, I thought it would be enlightening to examine Mexican laws regulating immigration and illegal immigration. Maybe we can learn something from our brothers to the south and adopt similar policies here.

According to Article 33 of the Mexican Constitution, "Foreigners may not in any way participate in the political affairs of the country." I assume this would include mass protests, political boycotts, illegal voting, and more. Good thing the US doesn't have such a law or we would have had to arrest about 100,000 people earlier this month.

Additionally, Article 27 states, "Only Mexicans by birth or naturalization … have the right to acquire ownership of lands, waters, and their appurtenances." Article 130 asserts, "To practice the ministry in any denomination in the United Mexican States it is necessary to be a Mexican by birth." And my favorite of all, Article 16 authorizes citizen arrests of any illegal immigrant by a Mexican citizen, stating "in cases of *flagrante delicto*, any person may arrest the offender and his accomplices, turning them over to the nearest authorities." In other words, every Mexican citizen has the legal authority to do exactly what the Minutemen are doing. Everyone in Mexico gets to be a "vigilante" to enforce immigration laws. Ironic then that President Fox would criticize our Minutemen.

The Mexican people also have the right idea when it comes to punishing violations of immigration laws. Their General Law on Population (*Ley General de Poblacion*) outlines the consequences. For starters, illegal immigration in Mexico is a felony. Article 123 tersely states, "A penalty of up to two years in prison and a fine of three to five thousand pesos will be imposed on the foreigner who enters the country illegally." Article 118 levies a harsher punishment on repeat offenders authorizing a 10 year jail sentence for people who re-enter the country after deportation. Articles 119–121 impose a six year jail term on foreigners who violate the terms of their visas. And Article 127 imposes a five year jail term on a Mexican who marries a foreigner with the sole objective of helping the foreigner live in Mexico.

After researching Mexico's laws on illegal immigration I was not surprised at what I found. It turns out that Mexico has a terrible problem with illegal immigration *on their southern border*. Immigrants from El Salvador and other Latin American countries constantly stream over the border. The Mexican government and the Mexican people feel they need to protect the integrity of their borders and, if necessary, employ harsh measures to secure them. What is puzzling is their reaction to our extremely lenient laws and lax enforcement. How can President Fox criticize American policy towards illegal immigration when it is far more humane than his own?

What I would love to see is thousands of Salvadoran, Bolivian, and Honduran illegal immigrants in Mexico plan a nationwide boycott and then take to the streets demanding that the Mexican government adopt immigration laws similar to those in the US. Or, all the illegal immigrants already here could go home and protest in front of their own government to demand fairer immigration laws from their country. That would make a little more sense than what I saw take place in the streets of America last month.

◆   ◆   ◆

There is an old saying that goes something to the effect of "you can take the boy out of the country but you can't take the country out of the boy." The same is true for teachers. We can change jobs, we can retire, but we never stop trying to educate people. It just becomes part of who we are. As a result, a lot of my columns and op-ed pieces are attempts to educate citizens on complex policy issues.

There aren't many policy issues more complex than health care. Almost every American has an opinion about what is wrong with our health care system, but very few have any good ideas on how to fix it. This occurs because only a handful of people actually understand WHY our health care system has problems. It's kind of like when your car breaks down. You know the car is not running. You know you are unhappy about it. But, unless you know why the car is not running, you can't do anything to remedy the situation. You end up going to a car repair guy and saying something really articulate like "Uhh, my car is making a funny gurgling noise." Oh that helps.

Rather than be the one millionth guy who tried to propose a solution to our health care "crisis", I instead attempted to educate people on the reason our health care system had problems. Through a series of analogies that simplified the issue, I argued that health care is expensive because of the way we buy and sell it, not because of "evil insurance companies" or "heartless Republicans." I wrote "Heath Care Costs without the Demagoguery" just after the scandal at Walter Reed Hospital broke in the media. For those who don't remember, the media discovered that many of our Iraq war veterans were getting terrible health care at the government run Walter Reed. I wrote a column with a different take than the mainstream media. I essentially said, "Of course the health care at Walter Reed is bad, it's run by the government. What else should we expect? The government doesn't do simple things well, what makes us think they would do complex things like health care any better?"

That didn't go over too well with my liberal neighbors and they lit into me with letters to the editor. Most of them extolled the virtues of socialized medicine. Others commented on how capitalism corrupted our health care system. Rather than fire back, I tried to educate them.

◆   ◆   ◆

"Health Care Costs without the Demagoguery"

Last month I wrote about the inefficiencies of government run health care at Walter Reed Medical Center. And, like moths to a flame, everyone who doesn't understand health care policy felt compelled to display their ignorance in the form of letters to the editor. I actually believe that drawing these people into the open is a form of public service, but I rarely respond because dueling op-ed pieces seldom get us anywhere. However, the letter by Mr. Smith arguing that America's health care costs are high due to private sector overhead costs was so staggeringly off the mark it served two purposes. One, it gave me something to bring into my political economy class illustrating how little some Americans know about health care policy, and second, it drove me to write this essay.

Americans pay extremely high health care costs for three reasons: the way we buy health care, the way the government makes us sell health care, and who pays for health care. Let's start with the first.

Take a moment to think about the way you buy groceries. Everything you put in the basket you pay for. The more you put in, the more you pay. This is what keeps you from putting everything in the basket (and leaving some for others). But imagine if we changed that. Instead, at the first of each month you wrote one check for $250 to Fred Meyer and then you were allowed to shop as much as you want, as often as you want, and take whatever you wanted. Would your shopping habits change? Facing no incremental costs due to increased consumption, you would take more and more. Take the good beer. Take more beer than you need. Let's raid the electronics section. Who cares? Once you pre-paid your $250 you can take whatever you want without feeling any extra costs. Well, Fred Meyer would care and they would increase to $1000 your flat monthly fee, and then we would start complaining about the high cost of food. Democrats would start calling for national food insurance! This may sound crazy in the grocery industry, but it's exactly how we buy health care. It's why we don't ask doctors "how much is that x-ray?" In the short run, it doesn't matter. Nor does it matter if I go to the doctor once or ten times. The system encourages over-consumption until insurance companies have to raise premiums because of our shopping behavior.

Second, imagine a country that makes everyone buy a Mercedes-Benz for a car. It would be illegal to buy a Prius. Would people in this country have better cars? Yes. Would fewer people own cars? Absolutely. If we require that everyone buy a $60,000 car, fewer people will own them. This is how the government makes us sell health care. Our state legislature and our federal government create "mandates" in health care. They say "You must cover this, and you must cover that." Eventually, health care plans cover just about everything, but they also become extremely expensive. A 22-year-old male doesn't need the same coverage as a 60-year-old female, but the government doesn't give him the choice to buy a smaller plan. Facing the expense, he usually chooses not to buy health care at all. Many economically ignorant politicians (think Hillary) want to use government to make health care more affordable when government is the reason it costs so much! If government would allow private insurers to sell many levels of health care, just as Detroit sells many types of cars, we would all have health care ... just like we all have cars (even the poor).

And finally, who pays. The problem here is that everyone gets health care but not everyone pays. Go to the hospital. If you have no money, you still get admitted. So, we have a system where 100% of the people consume health care but maybe 75% pay for health care. That means your bill is about 25% higher than what you actually used. Your bill must compensate for the bills that aren't paid by others.

So there you have it. These are not the only three reasons, but they, along with high tort costs, are the main reasons that health care is so expensive. Now its time for everyone who didn't understand this essay to start writing letters to the editor.

◆   ◆   ◆

For me, everything always comes back to being a teacher. So I'm going to end this chapter with my thoughts on school reform. As someone who has spent most of my life in the arena of education, I can tell you that America's school system is not as bad as the critics and media make it out to be. Most children in this country get a good education at our public schools. There are, however, some serious problems we need to address.

First and foremost, we need to remember that it is okay to tell children they are wrong. Schools have become so caught up in being "sensitive" and ensuring that we don't harm students' "self-esteem" some teachers have forgotten that education is a process of learning correct from incorrect. If we don't tell students when they are wrong, they will never know when they are right. Secondly, children don't get self-esteem from a gold star on a bad paper. They get self-esteem from learning to do something well.

Schools also need to worry less about being "politically correct" and more about teaching basic skills. We have too many new teachers coming out of colleges of education that are way too liberal. When these teachers get their first jobs, they want to teach about "multiculturalism" and "diversity." They need to teach math. America used to produce great engineers. Now we import our engineers from China and India. I once attended a curriculum meeting and learned that one of the math books told children to "get in a group and write a song about *what it feels like* to be a denominator." Are you kidding me?! I don't give a hoot what it feels like to be a denominator. I want my kids to learn how to do division.

And finally, I believe the monopoly the National Education Association and other teachers' unions have over education is harmful to our children. Monopolies never work. Why would we expect an education monopoly to work? A little competition would go a long way to improving our school system. As a teacher who worked in both the public school system, the private school system, and for a charter school, I can tell you we need all three in America. Unions don't want charter schools because they see them as a threat to "their" funding. However, I have never met a confident teacher who was scared by a charter school. Only teachers who weren't very good at what they did feared charter schools. Bad teachers feel safe protected by unions. Good teachers accept a little healthy competition.

◆   ◆   ◆

"Confident Teachers Support Charter Schools"

I was profoundly saddened to hear that the Washington Education Association (WEA) plans to overturn the recently enacted charter school bill. Charter schools are an excellent way to provide specialized teaching environments to students who are often overlooked in mainstream classrooms. I know. I used to be a high school teacher and I founded a charter school designed to help at-risk students graduate. Running that charter school was like being in the Peace Corps. I was proud of the work I was doing, but the working conditions were pretty tough. In the first few months, we had to meet at the local park. Because our building wasn't ready yet we ran extension cords out of the bathrooms to power the computers (not exactly an Ivory Tower). All of our students had been expelled from the local high school or had come from juvenile hall. When I lectured to the class, it was like a Mormon missionary addressing a chain gang. But we all persevered and two years later, all but one of those students received a diploma or a GED. Looking back, I consider that charter school one of my greatest contributions to society.

But to the WEA, I'm the enemy. I made the classic mistake of putting the interests of my students ahead of the interests of my union. Teachers' unions are notorious for claiming to speak for the interests of students. Don't be fooled.

Teachers' unions are exactly what the title implies; unions to protect the interests of teachers. Otherwise, it would be called a student union. Not that there is anything wrong with a union for teachers. Teachers are hard working, dedicated people and they deserve to have an organization looking out for their interests. But their unions try to gain the support of voters by claiming to speak for the students. Teachers may speak to the interests of students, but their unions almost never do.

Teachers' unions fear charter schools because charter schools break the union's monopoly over education, but more importantly, their monopoly over the educational funding. Just as Bill Gates doesn't want Microsoft to face any competition, neither do the teachers' unions. But the union's fear of charter schools is misplaced. They should not view charter schools as competition, but as assistance and specialization. Charter schools don't steal students (as if students are the property of unions) but offer to meet the needs of students who are falling between the cracks in regular schools. Even the most dedicated teacher can't meet the needs of at-risk students, AP students, and special needs students all in the same classroom. Why not let charter schools ease the burden.

When I was a teacher, my principal came to me and said he would like to observe my class. But, he had to give me two weeks notice per union rules. I refused to set a date. I told him a confident teacher would allow the principal to stop by anytime, anyplace. I wanted to be a good teacher everyday, not just on the one day a year the principal stopped in. My point is that confident and competent teachers are not afraid of charter schools, a little healthy competition, or even accepting a little help. Only insecure teachers fear school reform. When I was running a charter school, all the other good teachers in the district were behind us 100%. They knew we were all fighting the same battle, just using different tools.

In the coming months, the 76,000 strong WEA is going to ask you, the voters of Washington, to abolish charter schools. They are going to put cute little children in their ads to convince you. As an ex-teacher, let me tell you, the best thing you can do to protect you're child's education is to ignore the WEA.

8

The War On Terror

The war on terror is an ambiguous phrase. Is it a war like the "war on drugs" where we can never really declare victory as long as one addict is still using? If victory in the war on terror is like that, will we never be allowed to claim victory as long as one terrorist is still dreaming of his seventy virgins waiting for him in Heaven? Or, is the war on terror more like the Cold War—a long drawn-out ideological battle interspersed with occasional military action? At least with the Cold War we could point to the fall of the Berlin Wall and the collapse of the U.S.S.R. and say "We won." What we'll never see is Osama bin Laden signing surrender documents on the deck of the battleship Missouri with General Mac-Arthur looking on.

The reality is war has become more complicated. It is rarely fought between uniform-wearing armies clashing in open battle. War has become sporadic but longer. It has moved underground until it emerges in our cities and backyards. The enemy is often hidden and among us. Capturing cities or destroying infrastructure no longer leads to victory.

A new type of war puts new tensions on political systems, even one as old and stable as the United States. Our Constitution was written at a time when we fought wars the old way. Now we are being required to fight a new war with an old document. Luckily for us, our Framers had great foresight and built enough flexibility into our grand charter that we have been able to adapt. President Bush has been the first president to inherit this new type of war and he has been required to make some Solomon-like decisions.

Are we to treat terrorists like criminals and try them in civilian courts? Or do we treat them like soldiers and hold them in prisoner of war camps until the war is over? What if the war is not over for sixty years? How do we protect our borders and our civil liberties at the same time? Do we tap phone calls coming in from

Afghanistan or let terrorists converse freely to plot the next 9/11? It is easy for the academic or ACLU staffer perched in the ivory tower to opine from on high. They can put on their cloak of moral superiority and demand we fight the war on terror using the Queensberry rules. Easy for them to say. They don't have to call the parents and children of the people who die. The President does. It is the absence of responsibility that leads to self-righteousness. Presidents don't have that luxury.

For the past half decade this country has been fighting about how we should fight. On the Left there is a desire to fight using strongly worded U.N. resolutions, group-hugs, and tofu. They want to bury their heads in the sand, pretend there is no enemy, moralistically thump their chest and demand that the President fight a war with one hand tied behind his back. Luckily, this fringe group has been roundly ignored ... unless you walk the halls of academia. Poor me.

In this chapter, I examine some of the decisions we have made during the war on terror, complimenting some, criticizing others, and offering a sharp dose of reality to anyone who thinks we can win this war and hold on to our Pollyanna innocence at the same time.

Two of the most controversial decisions the Bush Administration made during the initial stages of the war on terror was passing the Patriot Act and opening the Guantanamo Bay detention center. When I wrote "Common Sense and Guantanamo Bay" the media was full of recriminations because it had been discovered that interrogators at Guantanamo were using scantily clad women and Twinkies to get information out of the detainees. In the article I address the Left's hysteria about this facility and argue for its continued use.

◆   ◆   ◆

"Common Sense and Guantanamo Bay"

Some people never miss the chance to declare their moral superiority over the rest of us. I don't know why, but hyperbolic, self-aggrandizing self-righteousness irritates me more than most distasteful political behavior. In our latest bout of collective hand wringing, the news has been full of condemnations criticizing the way the US government has been interrogating terrorist suspects at Guantanamo Bay. From the intensity of the self-indulgent whining, you would think government agents had reconstructed the Hanoi Hilton and were sticking bamboo shafts under the fingernails of these well-meaning but misguided terrorists. The truth, however, is far more insidious than we could ever have imagined. Did you know they have documented cases from Guantanamo Bay where interrogators have used Twinkies and other forms of junk food to entice terror suspects to spill the beans? I know. Try to keep your revulsion in check and don't let your children read this article. It may be too much for them to bear at such a young age. But I'm afraid it gets even worse. Earlier this year, it was learned that female interrogators were showing up to the detention center scantily clad. Yes, folks, you heard it hear. Women dressing up in mini-skirts and tank-tops to get information from Muslim terrorists. When, my friends, will the horror end?

This week, we had to confront another crime against humanity. It appears that interrogators may have been handling the Koran inappropriately. Of course, for all its symbolic value, we are talking about paper with ink on it. We are not talking about someone being beaten, starved, or tortured. But who cares really. If it makes a sensational story where a news reporter gets to smugly spew pious condemnations and Democratic senators get to wax poetically about their own moral authority, it is news my friend.

There is irony here of course. A few years ago, $15,000 of taxpayer money was used by the NEA and a photographer named Andres Serrano to finance Piss Christ, a photograph of a crucifix submerged in human urine. The same crowd that was defending the display as "art" back then is currently "outraged" by the despicable treatment of the Koran.

Now Amnesty International has decided to join in the self-congratulatory posturing by calling Guantanamo Bay "the gulag of our time." They catalogue a host of heinous treatment which includes sleep depravation and psychological torture. Apparently anyone who has raised teenagers has been subjected to torture if we accept Amnesty International's definition. But to claim that Guantanamo Bay is the functional equivalent of a gulag is proof positive that we have become victims of our own psycho-babble. In the Soviet gulags thousands of political prisoners were systematically killed through starvation and beatings. In Cuba, prisoners are interrogated by mini-skirt wearing women. Ya, I see the connection. Let's bring these shameless women before the Nuremburg courts.

I often try to imagine how Amnesty International would like to see interrogations take place. I think it would go something like this:

Interrogator: Tell us who your associates are and what they are planning.
Terrorist: No.
Interrogator: Please.
Terrorist: No.
Interrogator: Pretty please.
Terrorist: No.
Interrogator: Well, this guy is just too tough of a nut to crack. Send him back to the spa where he can wait for his private jet ride back to Afghanistan. Bring in the next guy.

Or, here is the way most Democratic senators would like to see Guantanamo Bay run:

Interrogator: Tell us who your associates are and what they are planning.
Terrorist: No.
Interrogator: Don't make me go to the UN and get a resolution demanding you tell me.
Terrorist: You wouldn't dare!
Interrogator: I will. In fact, we may go for a Security Council resolution condemning the fact you're not talking.
Terrorist: OK, OK, I give. Here is what I know.

The reality is that you can't win a war fighting by the Queensbury rules. Just like criminals, terrorists don't walk into an interrogation room and simply tell you everything you want to know. You have to manipulate them. Just like cops do down at the precinct. Sometimes, cops lie to suspects. They tell them their partner "ratted" them out even when they haven't. Sometimes they apply emotional pressure by talking about a suspect's mother or children. Sometimes they apply psychological pressure by letting them sweat for a while or telling them they will get the needle if they don't confess. All of this is fair game when you are trying to save lives and protect a community. It is also fair game when you are trying to nab terror suspects and learn more about their organizations. In fact it is more than fair game, it is common sense.

◆   ◆   ◆

One thing I know I can always count on is liberals sticking their heads in the sand and pretending they can't see evil in the world. They can always see evil in America, but never abroad. When terrorists kill Americans, the true liberal always asks, "What did we do to deserve this?"

The other thing I know I can always count on is the tendency of Americans to forget. Maybe it's the MTV-30 second-attention span world we live in. But as soon as something falls off the 24-hour news shows, we tend to forget about it. I remember the day after a student at Virginia Tech killed over thirty students. My school was in a panic. What can we do about it? How can we prevent it here? We had big plans. We were going to hold public meetings, develop emergency plans, and more. A week later we weren't even talking about Virginia Tech.

Our ability to forget is both a boon and a curse. When we forget, we heal. When we forget, we loose our sense of priorities. It is that dichotomy that reminds me of a dinner I had with nationally noted author and radio show host Michael Medved. I had invited Mr. Medved to be the Lincoln Day Dinner speaker in 2007. He graciously accepted. During his speech he asked a very pointed question. "If on September 12th we had asked ONE THING of President Bush, what would it have been?" His answer of course is that we would have asked him to prevent another 9/11 or another terrorist attack on American soil.

And that is exactly what President Bush did for Americans. Politically, however, his success was both a blessing and a curse. The blessing is obvious. But the curse is that we started to forget. As horrific as 9/11 was, we started to forget. What terrorist threat? Do we really need Guantanamo Bay? Do we really need a Patriot Act? Do we really need wiretapping? These are the questions that only people in a safe society get to ask.

As we began to forget, Al Qaeda and other terrorist groups began to remind us. There was the Beslen school attack in the Russian Federation where 186 children were murdered. There were the Madrid bombings that killed 200. Then there were the London bombings that paralyzed a city and killed 50 more. None of these attacks happened on American soil, but they came about as Americans were debating whether to roll back the Patriot Act. Democrats wanted it repealed. Republicans wanted it made permanent. I argued they were both wrong in "Renewing the Patriot Act."

◆ ◆ ◆

"Renewing the Patriot Act"

The recent London subway bombings have served as a reminder that the "war on terror" is more than just a political phrase. It seems that our own success at preventing domestic terrorist attacks lulled the nation into a false sense of security. One of the dangers faced by all democracies is that we forget so easily. But the London bombings have returned our attention to many of the questions we were asking just after September 11th.

In the days following the September 11th attacks we openly wondered if we would see suicide bombings in the NY subways and restaurants. It never happened, and we soon turned our attention to the war in Afghanistan and Iraq. But now would be a good time to ask WHY the United States has been spared these types of attacks. Although the media rarely reminds us, there has not been a single terrorist attack on American soil since 9/11. We must be doing something right.

One of things we are doing right is the Patriot Act. The Patriot Act succeeded in updating our laws to be effective in a 21st century technological environment. Prior to the Patriot Act most of our anti-terrorism laws were written before the advent of email, cell phones, satellites, and phone cards. It was quite easy for terrorists to avoid surveillance by simply purchasing several disposable cell phones and using numerous Hotmail accounts. The Patriot Act also disposed of what the 9/11 Commission called "stove piping". Because of the abuses discovered in the post-Watergate era, the CIA and the FBI, along with other government policing agencies, were barred from sharing information. In essence the right hand was forbidden from telling the left hand what it was doing. The Patriot Act lets our alphabet soups finally speak to one another.

The Patriot Act also confronted the problem that law enforcement officials cannot prevent terrorism while being handicapped by the extensive due process restrictions we have in place for domestic criminal offenses. Our criminal court system with its copious due process requirements is designed to ensure fairness for defendants *after a crime has already been committed*. But one cannot fight terrorism by prosecuting individuals after they have killed hundreds of people, and most likely, themselves. So the Patriot Act gave law enforcement and judges more leeway when it came to collecting and introducing evidence.

Despite the fact that the Patriot Act has numerous judicial oversight provisions and multiple sunset provisions, ideologues and reactionaries immediately pounced on the law as an infringement upon civil liberties. The most popular attack was to criticize the provision that allowed FBI officials to look at library records. About a year ago, then Attorney General John Ashcraft admitted the provision had never been used. It didn't matter. The attacks continued despite the fact that no one could provide ANY evidence that the Patriot Act had been abused in any way. Today's Wall Street Journal makes exactly that point.

As I write, the House and Senate are engrossed in discussions as to whether they should renew the Patriot Act as is, scale back the Patriot Act, or expand the Patriot Act. There are those in Congress who want to eliminate many provisions and increase barriers for evidence collection. Other members want to make the Patriot Act permanent by eliminating all the sunshine provisions. Both are wrong. We need the Patriot Act. But no law should be permanent. It is a good idea to force Congress to re-visit laws as time passes. The "war on terror" won't be eternal and therefore, neither should the Patriot Act. Just as much of the law written during the Cold War became either obsolete, or obstructive, the anti-terror provisions may need to be eliminated or altered in the future.

One of the problems our government faces is that too many laws are permanent. Once we get a law or a new program, Congress almost never repeals it. Did you know we still have subsidies for mohair? Do you even know what mohair is? In 1954 mohair was used to produce military uniforms. As a result, it was deemed a "strategic commodity" and eligible for a subsidy. A few years later Dacron was invented and the US military stopped using mohair. But here we are 50 years later and we still subsidize mohair.

Imagine if EVERY law passed by Congress had a sunshine provision. First, we would have fewer laws. Second, we would have lower taxes. But most importantly, our legal system would evolve as time progressed. Which brings me back to the Patriot Act. We need the tools this law provides.... for now. We may not need them in the future. So Republicans are right when they seek to renew the Act. They are wrong in trying to eliminate the sunset clauses.

◆　　◆　　◆

The war on terror started with a very bipartisan feel. I will always hold a few pictures in my mind—the entire Congress singing "God Bless America" on the Capitol steps, Democratic Senator Tom Daschle hugging President Bush at a Presidential Address to a Joint Session of Congress, and my favorite, President Bush throwing out the first pitch at a Yankee game right after 9/11.

As it often does, tragedy brought us together. Politics pulled us back apart. It's the nature of our system. But at the height of the partisan attacks, I made an unlikely prediction. I argued that things would get better in the long run. In "A Bipartisan War on Terror" I argued that as soon as Democrats became responsible for the war, either with a presidential victory or recapturing a majority in Congress, they would see the war through a different lens. Here is what I predicted.

◆　　◆　　◆

"A Bipartisan War on Terror: Not Yet, But It's Coming"

There is an old saying in politics that goes "politics ends at the water's edge." It means that Democrats and Republicans may duke it out in the halls of Congress when it comes to taxes, health care, and education, but both parties will stand unified when it comes to foreign policy. During the heights of the Cold War, there was a consensus among political parties when it came to defense spending, opposing communism, and endorsing the "containment doctrine." Sure, there were times of partisan disagreement (the nuclear freeze, unilateral disarmament), but in general, both parties stood shoulder to shoulder on issues of national defense.

As many look around today, they ask themselves where this spirit has gone. We see Democrats ripping into the Bush Administration for the Patriot Act, Guantanamo Bay, Iraq, and nominations such as Alberto Gonzalez and John Bolton. It seems as if the notion of politics ending at the water's edge is in short supply. Some wonder if this partisan divide concerning foreign policy will ever end.

I don't wonder. I know it will. We simply have to look to history as our guide.

The notion that Republicans and Democrats were instantly unified on foreign policy during the Cold War is something we like to believe through the rose-colored tint of revisionist history. The truth, however, is less idealistic. When Truman came to office, and inherited a new, bi-polar, nuclear world, the Republican Party attacked him relentlessly. Everything that went wrong was Truman's fault. Every setback in the Cold War was the fault of Democrats. The absurdity of the attacks reached a pinnacle when Republicans accused Truman of "losing China." Now Truman no more "lost China" than the Greeks lost Atlantis.

But then something funny happened on the way to reaching a crescendo of partisan attacks. The Republican Party, lead by Dwight Eisenhower, won the presidency. The Republicans even took control of the House for two short years. And oh how one's perspective changes once you're on the inside looking out, rather than the outside looking in. Finding themselves responsible for crafting foreign policy rather than lobbing cheap shots at those who were, Republicans, almost overnight, became more understanding of Truman's dilemmas.

And the exact same thing is going to happen (eventually) when Democrats win back the White House. Either in 2008 or some time after that, a Democrat is going to be elected president. And when that happens, Democrats will be responsible for keeping Americans safe. At which time, the Patriot Act is going to start to seem much more like a valuable tool for fighting terrorism than an infringement on civil liberties. Guantanamo Bay is going to become a practical and reasonable place to keep dangerous men, rather than the "gulag of our time." What happened to Republicans in 1952 is going to happen to Democrats in 2008 or 2012. Burdened by the responsibility of actually governing, they will no longer have the luxury of lobbing petulant cheap shots. Self-righteous whining will have to give way to making hard decisions that affect the security of millions of Americans.

And what will the Republicans be able to say? Nothing. Republicans, having drafted the Patriot Act, and created Guantanamo Bay, will look like hypocrites if they subject Democrats to the same type of criticism Democrats tossed at them. Conversely, Democrats, being forced to confront the same issues the Bush Administration did, will have a greater sense of understanding and empathy. The end result will be that the partisan intensity over the "war on terror" will abate. Once again, you will hear representatives from both parties talking about how "politics ends at the water's edge." But as before, it will not occur due to a sense of bipartisanship but a realization that the "tools" you criticize others for using may end up in your own "tool box" down the road.

It's kind of like how Yankee's fans hated Roger Clemens.... until he got traded.... to the Yankees.

◆　　◆　　◆

In this article, history proved me to be a little bit too pessimistic. I thought the Democrats would come around in 2008 or later. In truth, they came around a little earlier. As most of us remember, the Democrats rode a landslide to victory in the 2006 elections. They took control of the House and the Senate and won over many state legislative bodies as well. As expected, they engaged in some silly partisan legislation such as impeachment threats, symbolic labor bills, and some no-chance-in-hell Iraq measures. But after they settled down they woke up to find they were partially responsible for protecting the American people. Symbolism and vitriolic rhetoric would do any more. After spending the previous six year criticizing President Bush for the Patriot Act and domestic wiretapping, what did they do? They EXPANDED the President's domestic spying ability. An August 3rd, 2007 NY Times article noted, "[The] Senate approved a measure that would temporarily give the administration more latitude to eavesdrop *without court warrants* on foreign communications that it suspects may be tied to terrorism." Ah how the tables turn when you actually have to govern rather than simply stand on the sidelines and serve as her majesty's loyal opposition!

I'm going to end this chapter with the second most widely read article I ever wrote. In early 2007 I was invited to speak at the Cascadia Conference, a political conference put on by The Mainstream Republicans of Washington. The group is led by ex-Congressman Sid Morrison and other notable mainstreamers like Secretary of State Sam Reed. I was asked to speak about Iraq.

Wow. That is a big topic. What aspect of Iraq should I talk about, I asked. Whatever I would like was the response. I suggested a friendly critique of the war that suggested the much maligned neo-cons got some things right and some things wrong. The key to my argument was that democracy would not solve as many problems in the world as we think, but liberty will. A murky thesis to say the least, but I thought I could pull it off.

What makes the story interesting is that unbeknownst to me, Bruce Ramsey of the *Seattle Times* editorial page was sitting in the audience. He found my talk interesting and suggested to his colleagues that I submit a guest editorial to the *Seattle Times*. They liked the idea and the "rest is history" as they say.

"Liberty: A Capital Idea" is the only article I have ever written for a nationally known newspaper. I made many predictions in this article and I think it will be fun to pick up this book in ten years and see if I got any of them right. If I don't, it won't be so fun.

◆   ◆   ◆

"Liberty: A Capital Idea"

During a recent visit to Seattle, I encountered a young woman standing on a street corner demanding that President Bush take action to stop the genocide in Sudan. When I asked her if she thought Bush should send troops to the region as he did in Iraq, she responded with a blank stare. It was then that I realized she had not thought that far down the road. Although she wanted to use American power to stop genocide, she did not want to get her hands dirty accomplishing the task.

Dilemmas like hers are why I often remind my students and colleagues that only the impotent and the naïve have the luxury of self-righteousness. After our five-year experience in Iraq, Americans are also learning this lesson.

As a nation, we have messianic tendencies. We want to make the world a better place, but we often recoil at the real-world consequences of pursuing such policies. Our experience in Iraq requires us to re-examine the practicality of our goals and tactics, and ask ourselves what we might do differently in the future when we will most assuredly be needed to again intervene abroad.

I want to start with a relatively controversial premise. Despite the continual barrage of attacks from the blogging left, the neoconservatives got one core argument correct: Killing Osama bin Laden will do nothing to stop terrorism. If we want to stop terrorism, they correctly argue, we need to bring hope, social and economic mobility, and the rule of law to the places that foster terrorism. The mistake the neocons made was assuming that democracy would foster such an environment in the Middle East.

There are two reasons why initiating democracy early will not bring economic, social or political stability to the Middle East. First, democracy only works in places where it doesn't matter if you lose. Second, democracy does not bring about liberty. Liberty, though, may bring about democracy. Let's start with the first argument.

Democracy works in America because our lives are not dramatically altered in any way if our preferred candidate loses.

Would my life really be that much different if Al Gore had won in 2000 or John Kerry in 2004? Not really. My taxes would be a little higher. The regulatory state would be a little bigger, and heath care would be a little more bureaucratic. But the more fundamental aspects of my life, such as my job, my religion and my personal security, would be the same.

American elections don't lead to violence because although we fight so hard, we fight over differences that are minimal. I care if my taxes are 33 percent instead of 39 percent, but I won't kill someone over it. Can we say the same thing about democracy for the Hutus and the Tutsis in Rwanda or the people of Nigeria? Democracy doesn't work in some of these places because it matters if you lose. If you lose, you may have all your property taken, or worse, you die.

Turkey is currently learning the same lesson. As long as they only had secular candidates on the ballot, it didn't really matter who won or lost. Turkey would still be Turkey. Only life on the margin would change. When an Islamic candidate made the ballot, however, the Turks realized it would matter if the secular party lost. Their entire way of life might change. So they stripped that candidate from the ballot. Democratic? No. Good idea? Yes.

On the second point, the neocons assumed that democracy fosters liberty. They got it exactly backwards. Democracy doesn't foster liberty. Liberty, from time to time, fosters democracy.

Democracy does not cultivate liberty because democracy trades tyranny of the one for tyranny of the 51 percent. It does nothing to limit the power of government, protect the rights of minorities, or establish the rule of law. Democracy ends up looking just as ruthless as a dictatorship because it transfers ultimate and unchecked power from one to anyone who can create a coalition of 51 percent. In such a democracy, the other 49 percent usually pick up a gun. Take Afghanistan for example. The Taliban keep losing elections, but these losses do little to stop them from killing people.

The neocons were correct to start with their initial premise: Liberty will nurture an environment hostile to radical Islam. From there, however, they should have done a better job finding the variable that actually creates liberty. If they had looked harder, they would have found capitalism, not democracy.

Although there are always exceptions to the rule, history has shown that capitalism (more so than democracy) does an excellent job of fostering property rights, independent courts, the rule of law, and dispersing power to multiple stakeholders—particularly in countries that have few cultural predispositions toward civil society. We political scientists refer to these characteristics collectively as limited government. And a government with limited power is the government with the limited ability to kill its citizens, strip them of their resources, and deprive them of their liberty.

By comparing the development of Africa to Asia, we find support for this thesis. Africa's revolutions ushered in democracy overnight. They also ushered in ethnic fighting, genocide and civil war. Africa got democracy, but it couldn't find liberty. Asia, on the other hand, developed "authoritarian capitalism," which has slowly moved South Korea, Taiwan and Indonesia toward stable democracies. But capitalism and an independent, stable middle class that demanded limits on the reach of majority rule came first.

Russia and China offer an ongoing test of this process. Which one will be a freer society in 10 years? My money is on China. Russia hurried headlong into democracy. Now it has little more than a kleptocracy. China, which has moved to capitalism but not democracy, is emerging as the freer society.

My mother often repeats the phrase, "Don't throw the baby out with the bathwater." I think that would be good advice for us all as we assess where we are in Iraq, what we did well, and what we should do better if there is ever a "next time."

On the left, there should be acceptance that America does have a role in promoting environments that deter the development of radical and hostile ideologies. No nation that claims to walk in the light can ignore cultures that use children as bombs. In confronting these cultures, we may need to get our hands dirty, even act unilaterally, and especially have the patience to pursue foreign policies that bear fruit over generations, not 24-hour news cycles.

On the right, however, there must be an acceptance that democracy is not the panacea we would like it to be.

The difficulty facing the next president will be rallying the citizenry to a new noble cause, and then having to convince people that the noble cause may initially require an economic solution, not a political solution—a task made more difficult by the fact that democracy holds a softer spot in our hearts and is more amenable to lofty and passionate rhetoric than something so pedestrian as economics.

9

Free Markets And Free Trade

The thing I like about "free markets" and "free trade" is the "free" part. Markets and trade are the only mechanism mankind has ever crafted that organizes billions of people, moves goods and services all over the globe, increases the standard of living, and paves the way for peace and stability without forcing a single person to do anything they don't want to do. Markets and trade create wealth and liberty and they do it without an ounce of coercion. Everything in a market is voluntary. No one forces you to buy anything. No one forces you to produce anything. If you get rich in a market system, it is because people GAVE you their money. If you get rich in a socialist system, it's because you TOOK someone's money. That single difference is what makes markets a moral system and bureaucratic systems nothing more than legalized theft.

The other thing I like about free markets and free trade is that they *work*. Socialism doesn't work. Communism didn't work. Markets work. I often tell my students that the world fought an 80-year "battle of ideas" over who and what should control the actions of mankind. On one side we had the Karl Marx/John Keynes/Government side and on the other we had the

Adam Smith/F.A. Hayek/Milton Freidman/Market side. The market side won. The good guys won. Communism collapsed. Globalization and markets spread. East Germans moved west, not the other way around. Ireland is mimicking Reaganomics. No one is mimicking Marx. Well, I shouldn't say that. There are three places in the world that still hold to the view of Karl Marx: Cuba, North Korea, and Sociology departments in American universities.

When I was the guest speaker at the Discovery Institute's Slade Gorton Lecture Series in Seattle, Washington, I was asked what I would do to change the State Legislature. I said I would go to Olympia and pass out Economics 101 textbooks to every member of the House and Senate. I also said I would stand outside on the corner and hold up a big poster of a supply and demand curve yelling, "This is a supply and demand curve. Learn it. Love it. Obey it." I should note I had a few cups of coffee that afternoon.

I admit I am an unabashed crusader when it comes to educating people about markets and trade. I honestly believe that if I could educate liberals with regards to how markets work, why messing with them always makes things worse, and how free trade and open markets will bring about a world without war, I would die a happy man. Unfortunately, at the rate things are going … I can never die.

So, I have saved the chapter about markets and trade for the last. Kind of like dessert. Except that I have a sister-in-law that always eats her dessert first. She says, "Life is uncertain. Eat dessert first." If you are like my sister-in-law, you should have read this chapter first.

The other warning I will give you is this: free markets and free trade are not intuitive concepts. You'll have to think a little harder to understand this chapter.

◆   ◆   ◆

"CAFTA: The Complex Benefits of Free Trade"

It is always a great day in American politics when elected officials do the right thing even in the face of vitriolic opposition. Case in point: President Bush signed the Central American Free Trade Agreement this month over the objections of passionate but misguided detractors. The treaty represents a significant victory for the American economy, even if many citizens don't realize it.

Free trade is one of those issues that is incredibly complex, overwhelmingly beneficial, but regularly demonized by those who don't understand it. Unfortunately, too many Americans don't comprehend the complexities of Ricardian economics and oppose free trade out of ignorance or misinformation. But free trade, like quantum mechanics, works whether we understand it or not. Here is what we know.

Free trade creates jobs. The Commerce Department under President Clinton reported that NAFTA resulted in a net increase of 160,000 new jobs. Later studies put the figure much higher (in the millions). The problem with free trade isn't economics, it's politics. Free trade offers huge long-term benefits with some minimal short-term costs. What democracies prefer, however, are immediate benefits and no costs whatsoever. We vote in two-year cycles and we want results even faster. But good economic policy takes patience.

We know protectionism fails. Just ask President Bush. Prior to the 2004 election he slapped steel tariffs on foreign importers to protect jobs in politically sensitive Ohio. And it backfired. For every job he protected in Ohio, he lost two jobs in other sectors that purchased steel, like the construction industry in Florida and the auto industry in Illinois. When jobs started evaporating faster than they were being protected, Bush got a quick lesson in Ricardian economics and the tariffs quietly expired.

But if free trade is so beneficial, why are some people doggedly opposed to it? The answer lies in how free trade is advantageous. Beneficial policies can be grouped into two categories: Pareto efficient and Kaldor-Hicks efficient. When a policy is Pareto efficient there are some "winners" but no "losers." Pareto efficient policies almost always pass because the winners fight for them and, absent any losers, there is little political opposition. Kaldor-Hicks efficient policies, however, have winners and losers, but the winners win more than the losers lose (Still with me?). Imagine a society of 10 people where seven people "win" a dollar and three people "lose" a dollar. In all, the gains are larger than the losses and governments could institute a policy where the winners compensate the losers and still come out $4 ahead (e.g. the winners pay higher taxes to pay for job retraining for the losers). Free trade is a Kaldor-Hicks efficient policy.

Unfortunately, Kaldor-Hicks efficient policies run up against another political phenomenon know as "asymmetry of incentives," in this case something called "concentrated pains and diffused benefits." An asymmetry of incentive occurs when some people have a larger incentive to fight than others (remember Vietnam?). For example, imagine a policy where one million people will gain $100 but 500 people will lose $10,000. The 500 losers are going to intensely oppose this policy. But the one million winners are not going to "go to the mat" to fight for their $100. In the end, the "squeaky wheel gets the oil" and the attention of politicians. The policy dies, even though such a policy would have added almost $100 million dollars to the economy. The same thing happens with free trade. NAFTA created millions of new jobs and caused the loss of thousands of other jobs. But the job losses were concentrated in a few sectors of the economy (textiles in North Carolina) and the job gains were diffused over 150 million employees. The huge number of job winners didn't associate their gains with NAFTA and quietly went to work, but the small number of job losers did make the association and loudly made trade a campaign issue and economic villain.

Understanding the concept of "concentrated pains and diffused benefits" also explains why presidents from both parties always support free trade, but particular members of Congress oppose it. Presidents represent the whole country which receives the "diffused benefits." Members of Congress represent small segments of the nation, some of which are experiencing the "concentrated pains."

◆　　　◆　　　◆

When my CAFTA column came out, it was one of those few articles that was distributed across the state. As such, I got a wider audience but also a lot more feedback, much of it negative. I was expecting this. I live in a state that has a place called Seattle. Seattle is a place where in 1999, thousands of people wearing Nike shoes (which are produced with materials from around the world), toted cell phones (which are produced with parts from around the world) threw rocks (which come from all over the world) through the windows of Starbucks cafes to express their dislike for the World Trade Organization, globalization, free trade, and prosperity in general. On the ironic side, many of these ignorant protesters became acquainted with pepper spray (which is produced from materials from around the world).

The most common criticism levied at my essay was that free trade hurts the environment. This notion is completely false, but it is a powerful argument against free trade none the less. The criticism of free trade prodded me into writing a response which I titled "Free Trade and a Cleaner Environment.

◆　　　◆　　　◆

"Free Trade and a Cleaner Environment"

I'm going to do two things in this column I haven't done before. First, I'm going to discuss the same topic I addressed last month: free trade. Second, I'm going to reply to a letter to the editor that was written in response to that column.

Last month, I explained how free trade, despite its complexity, is beneficial to all nations. A reader responded with one of the more common criticisms of free trade: that it hurts the environment. The "damaged environment" argument is effective because it strikes a cord with many voters. The flaw with the argument is that it is completely false. The reality is, nations that engage in free trade see an improvement in their environment, not deterioration.

A nation's environment never improves due to external foreign pressures (such as a treaty). There are no political payoffs for government leaders to enforce values that come from abroad. Why would an elected official in Indonesia spend scarce resources to appease American voters? First World nations may force Third World governments to adopt strict environmental laws, but these governments won't commit tax resources to enforce such laws. As a result, the laws are on the books with no inspectors to enforce them. In contrast, when a nation's own people start to exhort political pressure on their own elected officials, environmental laws get enforced.

And guess where that internal political pressure always comes from? The middle class. People in poverty don't push for environmental protection. They are more worried about putting food on the table. It is only after a person has a roof over his head, food in his stomach, and security from lawlessness, that he turns his attention to protecting the environment. The empirical record shows that a nation's environmental movement is always tied to a rise in the middle class. It's an uncomfortable fact, but rich countries protect the environment, poor countries don't.

Here's where free trade comes in again. Rich countries trade. Poor countries don't. Free trade leads to economic growth, a higher standard of living, and the development of that crucial middle class. It is the emerging middle class that begins to engage politically, forming interest groups and social movements that push environmentalism. China, for example, has never had an environmental movement until just recently. China was bogged down in poverty and its citizens concentrated on feeding themselves. Then China joined the WTO, saw massive economic growth, and for the first time in its history, the newly created middle class started using violent demonstrations to demand environmental protections. In contrast, the nations that remain economically isolated have the world's worst environmental records.

Economists refer to this phenomenon as Kuznet curves. A Kuznet curve looks like a shallow "J" (a brief downturn followed by a steep upswing). Researchers have shown that nations which accept free trade experience a brief downturn in environmental standards followed by a long-term and significant improvement in environmental standards. Professors Jeff Frankel and Andrew Rose have shown that NO_2 and SO_2 decreases after nations adopt free trade policies. The World Development Report (1992) states, "The view that greater economic activity inevitably hurts the environment is based on static assumptions about technology, tastes and environmental investments" and that "as incomes rise, the demand for improvements in environmental quality will increase, as will the resources available for investment." Furthermore, Professors David Bradford and Stephan Shore show that once nations adopt free trade and see the development of a middle class, birth rates fall. The long-term result of lower birth rates is people do less harm to plant and animal habitats.

Liberals who oppose free trade on environmental grounds must face a difficult decision. They must decide if they truly want to help the environment, or, simply feel good about themselves. Those who only want to feel good about themselves, ignorantly participating in anti-free trade rhetoric, can continue with their same behavior. But those liberals who sincerely seek to help the world's environment must do the difficult thing and admit they were wrong. Let's hope they put the environment before their ego because their ego is standing between us and a cleaner world.

◆　　　◆　　　◆

I'm an optimist, even when it comes to thorny political issues. I often tell my students, "In the long run, good ideas push out bad ideas." Sometimes, the long run is just a little longer than I would like. I remind my students it took 80 years for the world to realize communism didn't work. Free trade didn't always have bipartisan support, but a consensus started to emerge in the 1990s.

Free trade is one of those issues that used to have only Republican support. The Democratic Party, with its support coming from labor unions, environmentalist, and consumer advocates has always been very wary of free trade. That all started to change when President Clinton finished the job President Bush Sr. started with NAFTA. Although I am often a critic of President Clinton, I always give him partial credit for two important policy developments of the 1990s: welfare reform and free trade. Clinton pulled his party to the middle and brought in some smart economic advisors who had the backbone to ignore the lunatic fringe of their own party. Men like Larry Summers and Robert Rubin saw the value in free trade and made sure Clinton did as well.

Unfortunately, a recent surge of "populism" in the Democratic Party has threatened our consensus on free trade. People like John Edwards play on fear and ignorance in an attempt to demonize free trade. Labor unions, flexing their muscle once again after the 2006 elections are demanding more trade restrictions. I fear the consensus is unraveling.

One of the easiest ways to attack free trade is to play on the biases and bigotry some people hold against "them foreigners." If an industry doesn't want to compete against India manufacturers, don't attack the products they sell, attack the people that produce them. One of the ugliest incidents involving a rejection of free trade happened a few years ago when our Congress demanded that we prevent a Dubai firm from managing one of our ports. It didn't matter that United Arab Emirates (UAE) is one of our closest allies, a moderate Middle Eastern state, and a loyal trading partner, their skin was a little too dark and manipulative senators saw an opening.

When the port deal failed, I took both parties to task: Democrats for their hypocrisy and Republicans for their cowardice.

◆   ◆   ◆

"Knee-Jerk Foreign Policy Coming to a Port near You"

When James Madison was designing the Constitution, he purposefully gave Senators longer terms than members of the House. He reasoned that officials with longer terms would be insulated from the instantaneous passions that culminate in a mob mentality. The Senate of today, however, led by hypocritical Democrats and cowardly Republicans is a mere shadow of the institution Mr. Madison designed so long ago.

Nothing could prove this point more than the disgraceful way our Congress managed the Dubai port deal. In an example of knee-jerk politics that ended in an orgy of xenophobia, our representatives offered up a plate of international public humiliation to one of our few allies in the Middle East. Not since Earl Warren and FDR started rounding up Japanese citizens in 1941 have we engaged in such open state-based bigotry.

What type of message does this send to the rest of the world? For the past few decades, the United States has been encouraging, cajoling, and invading countries in the Middle East in order to make them more moderate and market friendly. The United Arab Emirates (UAE) is exactly what we want Middle Eastern nations to look like. They support the US. They dock most of our naval ships. They reject Islamic extremism. 25,000 Americans live there and not one has been killed by a terrorist attack. Can we say the same of any other Middle Eastern nation? If all the Middle East was like the UAE, there would be no "clash of civilizations."

Foreign policy must be nuanced. At least, it must be more nuanced than "Europeans good … Arabs bad." As a nation, we must utilize sticks and carrots, not just sticks. Some Democrats think we should use only carrots. Some Republicans think we should use only sticks. Both are wrong. Long ago, economists learned that economic rewards will alter behavior far better than threats of fines. Any good parent or teacher knows that you can't just threaten to punish children to get them to behave. You also have to offer them rewards for being good. In the Middle East we **must** keep the gun loaded. But, we must also be willing to offer a hand of friendship to those who are willing to stand with us. Last week, we slapped the face of the few who have chosen to stand with us.

What caused this cacophony of bad policy? It was a combination of short-sided decisions. Democrats acted like hypocrites. The party that rejects racial profiling in the airport, arguing that grandma should be searched just as much as the middle aged Saudi male, now tells us that an entire nationality is unqualified to run a port. So eager to attack the President, they abandoned their historic commitment to civil rights in exchange for a few good days in the media. In their rush to the nearest microphone, both Senators Clinton and Schumer forgot to mention that a Saudi company (NSCSA) has been running the Brooklyn, NY ports for years.

Republicans fared no better. So afraid of giving up their advantage on national security issues, they were willing to fold like a cheap suit to appease angry voters. Not my definition of leadership. We need representatives who are willing to stand up to the instantaneously manufactured public opinion of talk radio.

Sometimes, leadership involves telling the people they are wrong. Not easy, but necessary.

President Bush was the only actor in this tragedy to put policy before polls. It is what has ingratiated him to many Americans. He does what he thinks is right, not what he thinks is popular. Doing so often makes him unpopular in the short run but admired in the long run. I think Mr. Madison was hoping we would have more people like that in the halls of Congress.

◆   ◆   ◆

Let's move on to free markets. One of the things I often tell policy makers is that the "invisible hand works fine without your help. If you mess with it, it will probably slap you upside the head." Not a diplomatic way to say something, but it is true. So many liberals want to "fix" the market, but like doctors who never studied anatomy, they usually don't understand the very system they seek to "fix" and end up making things worse. Most liberals live under the illusion that government can fix the market. In my experience, government can't fix a flat tire very well. I have no idea what would lead someone to believe government is the best tool to fix something as complicated as a market ... especially one that is not broke.

Like free trade, liberals are very good at demonizing the market. They throw around names like Enron, Exxon, and Dow Chemical to scare people into thinking that the government needs to continually protect us from the predatory market. I don't know about you, but I rarely need protecting from people who are falling all over each other to provide me with what I want. I always get a kick out of liberals who beat up on the insurance industry. You know, those terrible people who will rebuild my house if it burns down, replace my car if I get into an accident, and pay for my transplant if my heart goes bad. Damn those guys! Massachusetts liberals are my favorite. Out of one side of their mouth they demonize insurance companies and then they use the law to mandate that everyone buy the health insurance. Am I missing something here?

One of the great victories for markets in the past decade was when the Bush Administration reformed the Medicare system by using a market-based system to supply the elderly with prescription drugs. Rather than creating another cumbersome, impersonal, inefficient government bureaucracy, Bush set up a system where private drug companies had to compete for the business of Medicare patients. And it worked. The program is the only one I know of where after time, the amount of money being spent on it ... went down! Down? That is unheard of in government land.

The program's success however, did not insulate it from attacks from the Left. For some reason, the Left hates it when the market succeeds without the "help" of government. Maybe when this happens liberals and bureaucrats realize how much their "help" is not needed. As soon as the 2006 elections were done and we had to swallow the term "Speaker Pelosi," Democrats went to work unraveling the successful prescription drug program. They wanted government controls, mandates, and fixed pricing—essentially all the stuff people call for when they have never read that Economics 101 textbook I was talking about earlier. Lucky for the American people, their push failed, but I am sure they will try again. If they do, maybe I'll reprint "Bringing a Bad Idea to the Drug Market."

◆　　◆　　◆

"Bringing a Monopsony to the Drug Market ... and Other Bad Ideas by Nanci Pelosi"

I have been writing this column for the past four years. In that time, I have consistently emphasized how important it is for citizens to have a basic understanding of economics. In fact, you're probably sick of hearing it. But, as Democrats in Congress pursue an ill-conceived plan to require drug companies to negotiate with the government, never has my point been truer than now.

Like most poorly crafted economic policies, requiring direct negotiations between government and drug companies has support because a great majority of Americans have no working knowledge of how markets work, or how government can break them. They simply hear terms like "lower prices" and "greedy pharmaceutical company" and they jump on board. If Nanci Pelosi and her band of galloping ignoramuses get their way, we will see higher prices, more political influence by drug companies, and less medical innovation.

When the Bush Administration introduced the Medicare prescription drug plan the best part of the plan was to require markets to lower drug prices. And, it has worked exactly as planned. Drug companies are forced to compete for our business, offering individualized plans, incentives, and slashing prices. In fact, in the few short years the plan has been in action, the Medicare premium most elderly pay has fallen from $36 to $24 a month. How often have you seen governments take in less money? Other studies have shown that Americans, for the first time, are actually slowing the increase in health care costs … mostly due to lower drug prices.

But, when you demand that all drug companies negotiate with a single buyer, you introduce a monopsony into the market. A monopsony, although similar in concept to a monopoly, functions in a different manner. Rather than one seller, like a Rockefeller of old, you get one buyer. When everyone has to sell to the same buyer, there is no need to compete. No need to offer lower prices to gain more business. You simply accept the conditions and move on.

But worse than the destruction of incentives, a government regulated price system makes it easier for pharmaceutical companies to seize control of the very apparatus that sets their price. Economists call it "government capture." The beauty of markets is that they cannot be controlled or captured by anyone. There are millions of buyers and thousands of sellers. No one corporation can control them all. But, when a single entity like the FDA sets the price, it becomes very easy for drug companies to take over. Here is how it works.

All bureaucracies are controlled by "congressional oversight." This means that a handful of Congressmen get to set the direction of that bureaucracy (e.g. set drug prices). Unfortunately, corporations are very good at buying influence with elected representatives. It would be easy for a massive company like Glaxo to contribute enough money to control the 8-13 members of the Senate oversight committee. When they do, the government will miraculously decide to increase the payment to drug companies.

This story is old. We used to have a Civilian Aeronautics Board (CAB) in the US to "control prices" to "protect the consumer." However, the Board was controlled by Congress and large airline companies made sure that they contributed to the members that oversaw the CAB. As a result, flights were kept to a minimum and prices were purposefully kept high. When the CAB was disbanded in the 1970s (by President Carter) prices plummeted and the number of flights quadrupled.

The Bush Administration learned the lesson and prevented a similar gouging in 2002. Pelosi and company have not learned the lesson and now they appeal to a form of economic demagoguery. Pelosi knows she can use the economic ignorance of the American people against them. We all love to rally against those evil drug companies. What few understand is that if you want to control drug companies, and make them work for us, we should pit drug company against drug company, not bring them all into a smoke-filled room to collude with elected representatives they helped elect.

◆   ◆   ◆

Markets are impersonal. That is the criticism from some on the Left. I see it as a market's greatest strength. A market doesn't care if you are a man or a woman, if you are black or white, or if you are gay or straight. Wouldn't it be nice if the whole world worked that way? The reason I bring this up is that markets don't care what "product" is being "sold." A market will move a bar of soap just like it will move illegal drugs or cabbage patch dolls. I was struck by this fact when reading about the successes and failures various disaster relief agencies were having after Hurricane Katrina hit the Gulf Coast. Guess which groups did a better job bringing needed services to the victims—government agencies or private sector agencies?

◆   ◆   ◆

"Disaster Relief: Have you met the free market?"

In 1994, President Bill Clinton declared the "era of big government is over." After the New Deal, the Great Society, and eight years of Reagan and Thatcher proving that free markets do a better job of promoting prosperity than governments, it looked like we had finally learned our half century lesson.

But before the lesson could settle in, Hurricane Katrina brought winds, rains, and gale force stupidity. We actually have people asking if the "era of big government" should return proving that ideology typically trumps intelligence. After the complete failure of government bureaucracies to respond to hurricane Katrina, Democrats demanded.... pause.... wait for it.... .MORE GOVERNMENT!!

They completely failed to learn the true lesson of Katrina. That government is NOT the answer to most problems. As a comparison, look at how well the Red Cross and the Salvation Army responded to the crisis. Despite being non-profits, they are both market driven organizations. If they don't do a good job, people refuse to donate money to them. They were on the scene immediately. They didn't need 25 forms signed by 30 different government officials. While Gov. Kathleen Blanco, Mayor Ray Nagin and President Bush were debating who had the authority to help New Orleans, the private relief groups just acted. When the government finally got its ducks in a row, they decided the best way to help the people of the South was to suspend most of the government rules that people and business typically must follow. I guess it takes a national disaster to realize how burdensome most government regulations are.

Democrats also reacted by criticizing the Bush administration for not spending enough money on social programs and focusing too much on the war on terror. The truth is, the Bush administration has increased discretionary, non-defense spending by more than any other president since LBJ. According to the *Washington Monthly*, Bush has increased spending (adjusted for inflation) 8.2% compared to Carter's 2% and Clinton's 2.5%. But wait they say. It's not that you aren't spending enough money, it's that you aren't spending it correctly. That money should have gone to building better levees. All the reports indicated they were inadequate you know. Well, gee, do you think that maybe the problem was that environmental groups have prevented us from doing just that? The national Sierra Club was one of several environmental groups who sued the Army Corps of Engineers to stop a 1996 plan to raise and fortify Mississippi River levees. The Army Corps was planning to upgrade 303 miles of levees along the river in Louisiana, Mississippi, and Arkansas. According to Corps spokesmen "a failure could wreak catastrophic consequences on Louisiana and Mississippi which the states would be decades in overcoming, if they overcame them at all." But a suit filed by environmental groups at the U.S. District Court in New Orleans claimed the Corps had not looked at "the impact on bottomland hardwood wetlands."

But that is not the point. The real story is how over the moon, beyond comprehension, dim-witted the Democratic response has been. After seeing a complete failure in the way FEMA works they demanded.... pause.... wait for it.... MORE MONEY be given to FEMA. This is why government is such a miserable failure at most anything. They function under perverse incentives where failure is rewarded with larger budgets.

Can you imagine Bill Gates or any downtown merchant saying, "hey let's build a really crappy product so the consumers will give us more money to produce a better product the next time around?" No. In the free market, you build a better mousetrap or go out of business. In government, he who builds the most malfunctioning mousetrap gets the most tax dollars.

If we really wanted a more efficient and effective hurricane response system, the government should limit itself to creating a competitive grant program where private groups like the Red Cross could compete for federal dollars. The groups that do the best job helping the most people get the most grant money. I already have the motto for the new grant awarding bureaucracy: "The profit motive: working for you for the past half millennium."

◆   ◆   ◆

What's good for the goose is good for the gander. Just as free markets will do a better job than government when it comes to helping hurricane victims, markets will do a better job helping wounded war veterans when they get home. Once again to be filed in the "How Stupid Can You Be" folder, when the Walter Reed Hospital scandal broke a few years ago, Democrats attacked President Bush for the failure of this government run hospital, and then demanded we needed nationalized health care! Of course, one government run hospital is doing a terrible job, so let's make them ALL government run hospitals. I can't make this stuff up.

◆   ◆   ◆

"Learning the Wrong Lessons from Walter Reed"

Every once in a while a political scandal will come to light in which most Americans learn the entirely wrong lesson. The revelation of terrible medical care at Walter Reed hospital is a perfect example. While most Americans are sensibly outraged at the compassionless care our veterans are receiving, too many see these events as an isolated incident that can be overcome with more money and better management. Neither is correct. The problems at Walter Reed are systemic to all government run services and the lesson we should be taking from Walter Reed is "Thank God the Government Doesn't Run My Health Care!"

I always get a smirk on my face when someone (usually a liberal) spends a few minutes ranting at the Bush administration for its handling of Walter Reed and then in the next breath goes into a rant about how America needs a national health care system run by…. that's right, the same people running Walter Reed hospital. The only thing worse than letting the government run veteran health care would be to let the government run all health care. Government can't do simple things well, what makes anyone believe they can do complex things (like health care) well?

Walter Reed is not a disaster because the doctors there are incompetent or the nurses are indifferent. Walter Reed is a failure because it exists in a world absent of individual incentives and market forces. Walter Reed has the same level of customer service you will find at the DMV in Seattle. And for the same reason; no one has an incentive to do a better job. There are no repercussions for inexcusable service. Trust me, if the State of Washington were to seize control of the Kittitas Valley Community Hospital our medical service would be the same as our poor veterans are receiving. It doesn't matter how good the people are you put in a bad system, you will still get bad results. If you don't believe me, just check out the effectiveness of the United Nations or how compassionate the Internal Revenue "Service" can be.

In Olympia there are a variety of ill-conceived plans to let the state creep further into our health care system. In 2008, the presidential campaign is going to put nationalized health care front and center. If we want to look at the one example we have of real world state run heath care, we will be wise to remember the miserable failure the government has been at Walter Reed. My fear is that too many will be blinded by their animosity towards the Bush administration to learn the correct lesson from our experience.

While it is true that our current health care system is not perfect (mostly due to government mandates, not market failure) we should be loath to replace an imperfect system with a disastrous "Hillary-care" system. Most Americans receive pretty good health care. It is why many people with a state run heath care system come here for major surgery. In our desire to provide better health care for the 10% of people falling between the cracks, we should not destroy the excellent health care the other 90% is already getting. This is the danger of democracy that Alexis DeTocqueville warned us about. He observed that it always easier to push the top down than to pull the bottom up. Yes, there are uninsured Americans.

But, I am not willing to subject my wife, and everyone else I know, to the compassionless and disgraceful health care of Walter Reed, just to pull those 10% up.

10

The Last Word ... For Now

Where do we end a book like this? History continues to unfold as you read and I write. Politics moves on and new issues arise. There is always a place for more commentary.

I choose to end it with my favorite essay. Surprisingly, it is not an essay directly addressing politics but in its own way, is the best representation of my political views. It is simply titled "Graduation Day."

Graduation day is one of best things there is about being a teacher. You get to see your best work walk across the stage. No matter how many times I hear "pomp and circumstance," no matter how many commencement addresses I sit through that end with "God speed," and no matter how many times I go to the BBQs of proud parents, I never get cynical about the celebration of graduation day. It's the one day a year I get to pause and reflect on all that has been accomplished in the past year. Not enough jobs have a moment like that. For most careers, one day just blends into the next and then one project just blends into another. But people need finish lines even if there isn't a finish. For me, graduation day serves that purpose.

A few Junes ago, I wanted to write an essay for my students and to my students. I have a colleague who says we professors "do a lot of teaching but very little professing." I wanted to do a little professing. It was published a few days after another Central graduation. It was not picked up by the wires or any other newspaper. It didn't affect any presidential election. It did not generate a single letter to the editor. But, if I had to select the one essay that I have ever written as "my favorite" this would be the one. I hope you enjoy it.

◆   ◆   ◆

"Graduation Day"

Once a year, I dig into the very, very back of the closet to pull out my bright blue, overly ornate doctoral robes. When I have them on, I look more like Harry Potter than the monks of old, but it is the way I choose to celebrate one of our grandest traditions: graduation day.

As I walk around town, I am usually met with a variety of reactions. Children expect me to do magic tricks. Adults give me either a perplexed stare or a knowing nod. Some think I do it to be pretentious, and others wonder why an educated man would wear thick felt on a day that typically reaches 100 degrees.

I wear the robes for other reasons. I wear them because I believe it is important, in an age of increasing cynicism, to remind people of the importance of ceremony. When there is so much that divides us, it is important to maintain the vibrancy of the few rituals the unite us.

I think people are too quick to dismiss the pageantry of our customs today. We focus too much on the legalistic definition of marriage than the majesty of the wedding ceremony. We wonder too much what the diploma or degree is worth rather than the pomp and circumstance of the students marching in front of proud parents. The jaded curmudgeon scoffs at the State of the Union or Inaugural Address as a meaningless media event failing to appreciate the healing nature of national spectacles. Patriotism is too often discounted as jingoism. Ceremony is deconstructed as nothing more than manipulation.

But I believe there is something about the nature of ritual that is integral to the human condition. We need ceremony. We need it to remind us that there are ambitions that transcend the individual. We need it to remind ourselves that we are connected by time as much as geography. The pageantry of ritual places at the center of our consciousness the "ideal" that we so often forget as we daily confront the reality of our own shortcomings. As former governor Mario Cuomo said, "We campaign in poetry but we must govern in prose." I think he was right, and I don't have a problem with that. If we did both in "prose," what would we have to aspire to?

I think earlier generations had a better grasp on the importance of symbolism. They gave us the National Anthem, the Pledge of Allegiance, Memorial Day, Labor Day, the Presidential Seal, the White House and even unlikely stories of Washington chopping down a cherry tree. I don't think these people were naïve. Having lived through war, economic depression, and racial intolerance, they fully understood the reality of human existence. But, they also understood the importance of events and symbols that encourage us to put aside temporary partisan differences to focus on the larger issues that can create a nation out of a collection of individuals.

The month of graduation is a good time to make this point. Come September, I will be standing in front of too many students who are unjustifiably cynical. They will believe that every representative is corrupt, every national event is a conspiracy, and most of our history is an act of oppression. While it is our job as educators and parents to hold up an unflinching mirror to our society, it pains me to see so many people so cynical so soon. I don't know if there is much I can do to stem the tide. But for one day each year, whether it helps or not, I will be the guy in the dark blue robes, wandering the streets of Ellensburg, engaged in the pageantry of one.

978-0-595-46675-7
0-595-46675-3

LaVergne, TN USA
28 August 2009
156086LV00004B/14/A